STORM WARNING

STORM WARNING

Poets for the Planet Building Socialism

Revolutionary Poets Brigade

Edited by
Lisbit Bailey, Kristina Brown, Bobby Coleman,
John Curl, Karen Melander-Magoon

Copyright © 2022 by Kallatumba Press.

All rights reserved. No part of this book may be reproduced by any means, including information storage and retrieval or photocopying, except for short excerpts in critical articles, without written permission of the publisher. Intellectual property reverts back to the individual poets and translators upon publication.
ISBN: 978-0-938392-16-3

Kallatumba Press
San Francisco, CA

http://revolutionarypoetsbrigade.org/
Printed in the United States of America.

CONTENTS

PREFATORY ... 8

INDRAN AMIRTHANAYAGAM *(Sri Lanka)* ... 13
AYO AYOOLA-AMALE *(Nigeria)* ... 15
MAHNAZ BAHIDIAN *(USA/Iran)* ... 16
LISBIT BAILEY ... 17
KEMLYN TAN BAPPE ... 20
VIRGINIA BARRETT ... 23
JUDITH AYN BERNHARD ... 25
SCOTT BIRD ... 26
CHARLES CURTIS BLACKWELL ... 27
DAN BRADY ... 28
DANIEL BROOKS ... 29
KRISTINA BROWN ... 30
JEREMY CANTOR ... 33
YOLANDA CATZALCO ... 34
MARCO CINQUE *(Italy)* ... 38
BOBBY COLEMAN ... 43
FRANCES COMBES *(France)* ... 44
KITTY COSTELLO ... 48
J. VERN CROMARTIE ... 49
ANITA CRUZ ... 51
ROMEO CRUZ ... 52
JOHN CURL ... 54
AMIT DAHIYABADSHAH *(India)* ... 55
CAROL DENNEY ... 56
GERMAIN DROOGENBROODT *(Belgium)*... 57
CARLOS RAÚL DUFFLAR ... 58
MARIA J. ESTRADA ... 60
AGNETA FALK ... 61
MAURO FFORTISSIMO ... 63
MARK FISHBEIN ... 65
MARCOS DE SOUSA FREITAS *(Brazil)* ... 66

RAFAEL JESÚS GONZÁLEZ *(USA/Mexico)* ... 70
ART GOODTIMES ... 72
EGON GÜNTHER *(Germany)* ... 74
JACK HIRSCHMAN ... 76
EVERETT HOAGLAND ... 77
ANTONELLA IASCHI *(Italy)* ... 78
BRUCE ISAACSON ... 80
ZIBA KARBASSI *(Iran)* ... 82
ELIOT KATZ ... 86
D.L. LANG ... 88
ANN LEONARD ... 90
GENNY LIM ... 93
MARK LIPMAN ... 95
ANGELINA LLONGUERAS *(Catalonia)* ... 96
OSCAR LOCATELLI *(Italy)* ... 98
ANNA LOMBARDO *(Italy)* ... 100
KIRK LUMPKIN ... 104
JUAN ALCALA LUNA ... 107
BIPLAB MAJEE *(India)* ... 108
devorah major ... 110
AHCENE MARICHE *(Algeria)* ... 112
ÁNGEL L. MARTÍNEZ ... 117
ALBERTO MASALA *(Italy)* ... 118
TOMMI AVICOLLI MECCA ... 124
KAREN MELANDER-MAGOON ... 125
SARAH MENEFEE ... 126
TUREEDA MIKELL ... 128
GAIL MITCHELL ... 132
EDWARD MYCUE ... 133
MAJID NAFICY ... 134
BILL NEVINS ... 135
DOROTHY (DOTTIE) PAYNE ... 136
POET E SPOKEN ... 139
GREGORY POND ... 141
KATHY POWERS ... 143

THORWALD PROLL *(Germany)* ... 144
SANDRO SARDELLA *(Italy)* ... 146
LUIS FILIPE SARMENTO *(Portugal)* ... 152
NINA SERRANO ... 154
KIM SHUCK ... 155
DINO SIOTIS *(Greece)* ... 156
DOREEN STOCK ... 158
SARAH THILYKOU *(Greece)* ... 160
MATTHEW TALEBI ... 163
RAYMOND NAT TURNER ... 164
DAVID VOLPENDESTA ... 166
OSCAR SAAVEDRA VILLARROEL *(Chile)* ... 168
CATHLEEN WILLIAMS ... 169
D.A. "ROARSHOCK" WILSON ... 171
XIAO-XIAO *(China)* ... 174
ANDRENA ZAWIN SKI ... 176

BIOGRAPHIC NOTES ... 178

VISUAL ARTISTS

Front Cover: Ronald F. Sauer.
Back Cover: *"Web Of People, Bahia"* Seed panel of the VI Agroecology Day in Bahia: collective production under the guidance of Maritania Andretta Risso.
Cover Design: Scott Bird.
p. 9:   Catherine Karpow
P. 14: Sandro Sardella.
P. 19: Kemlyn Tan Bappe, *"Two Tigers."*
P. 42: Agneta Falk.
P. 116: Roger Strobel.
P. 162: Sandro Sardella.

PREFATORY

It's Spring 2022. The time of Earth Day, Equinox, and Renewal. The COVID pandemic has been downgraded to an endemic after more than two years. Democracy is under unprecedented attack around the world. Russia is at war with Ukraine.

At this perilous moment, the Revolutionary Poets Brigade presents our eleventh international anthology: *Storm Warning: Poets for the Planet Building Socialism*. *Storm Warning* contains auguries of struggle for a just and sustainable world in a precarious future that has already begun with rising sea level, drastic changes to local climates, ever more extreme weather events, chronic drought, flooding, lengthening fire seasons, and countless other environmental disasters. The global focus of these poems is on climate change, planetary warming, environmental resistance, and social justice, all driven by the aggression and arrogance of Capitalism and evermore evident Fascism.

This anthology differs palpably from the previous ten. Most significantly, it's the first prepared without Jack Hirschman. Jack said, "Everyone's a poet." To him, creating, sharing, and reading poems out loud are revolutionary acts. Each poem calls to everyone everywhere to find the poet within, rediscover our shared humanity, and envision a future where our natural environment is cherished, and everyone's basic needs are met. As poets, it's our responsibility to use our poetic power for the stewardship of our Mother Earth and all who live here.

Many hands make up the cadre that has brought this anthology to life, but the Revolutionary Poets Brigade and this continuing anthology series would not have brought us together without Jack's deep love and belief in each one of us.

Jack Hirschman presente!

Editors
Lisbit Bailey, Kristina Brown, Bobby Coleman, John Curl, Karen Melander-Magoon

Jack Hirschman at Caffe Trieste.
photo credt: Catherine Karpow

STORM WARNING

INDRAN AMIRTHANAYAGAM *(Sri Lanka)*

FIN DE SIÈCLE MEDITATION

Minor not mynah, small not full-frontal
cawing, chamber not ninth symphony,
what you write in the workshop, carving
on a cup, man on a mountain, Japanese
and Chinese aesthetic, but then Genji
appears and speaks through a thousand
screens in the imperial court, and Gilgamesh
swags on the high seas, Odysseus sails from
the burning tower, the Mahabharata, game
of dice that will determine existence
or disappearance, every culture its epic,
every culture its whisper, every culture
fiddling while it burns, turning away
from the stage saying never more.

Sandro Sardella

AYO AYOOLA-AMALE

WE ARE EARTH

The Earth,
Our mother calls us
with her outstretched arms
To restore our peace, to heal us from wounds
To bring back our joy from woes.
Away from numb forests crowning the town
death choirs, rotten skeletons struggling dust load.
The Earth knows all about us
ransomed to death,
about how our mind made shackles
about how we depend on her as deep breath flowing out
Land ruin, decayed souls stand in the long streets, walls
we must stop wars
we must stop heating the earth, ecosystem mouthings
of wide-leg tulip pants on dead mountains
hut howls,
of afflictions with pandemics-
the conjugal cemetery, plagues
drunken capitalist beasts breeding
loss and inequality like fire burning souls,
of deep reckless assault,
our extinction
our irresponsibility is like with yellow taxicab noises
filled with babies on a ride to the beach of desert sand
                                                                      dunes

the ones that exist and the ones that don't exist.
A making all-true
that always say something deep.

MAHNAZ BAHIDIAN

IMAGINE

Imagine that every morning on every door
A stem of a flower, of love, hangs
void of locks, chains, and iron fences.
And every day on the streets,
children play like free birds.
Hand in hand with full bellies
with the right shoes on their feet
going to school,
without fear of being stolen.

Dogs and cats like dear citizens,
walk with patient men and women

We can imagine that we all can
live Together
without war and bloodshed,
Wherein people shall worship
the earth and the lands.

A world in which every human death
would be a disaster.
And in it, there will be fruits,
and trees and plants,
In place of cannons and guns
Anthem and poetry in place of anger and hostility

LISBIT BAILEY

AS THE MANTA RAYS DANCED

To Mother Earth:

your heart is immortal!
wind is your breath

water is your blood
land is your flesh

springing to life again
you divined us - the "doubly wise man"

a brimming rebirth
our needs fulfilled by your gifts

we feasted on fishes and beasts
as the manta rays were dancing in your brine

lulled by your rhythms
we believed your meandering was indifference

we flowed over you
thirsty for more

we colonized, industrialized
invented the quackery of race

in a millennial moment
we seeped into your breath, blood and flesh

algae, coral and kelp ebbing in your seas
plankton imbibing micro-plastics in your abyss

extreme weather is your May Day
while "doubly wise" man is in control

still we refute our influence
invent ways of rescuing you for material gain

we pour down on you
but you've survived extinctions

Mother Earth! Divert the reservoir of your strength
so the oceans will dance with life again!

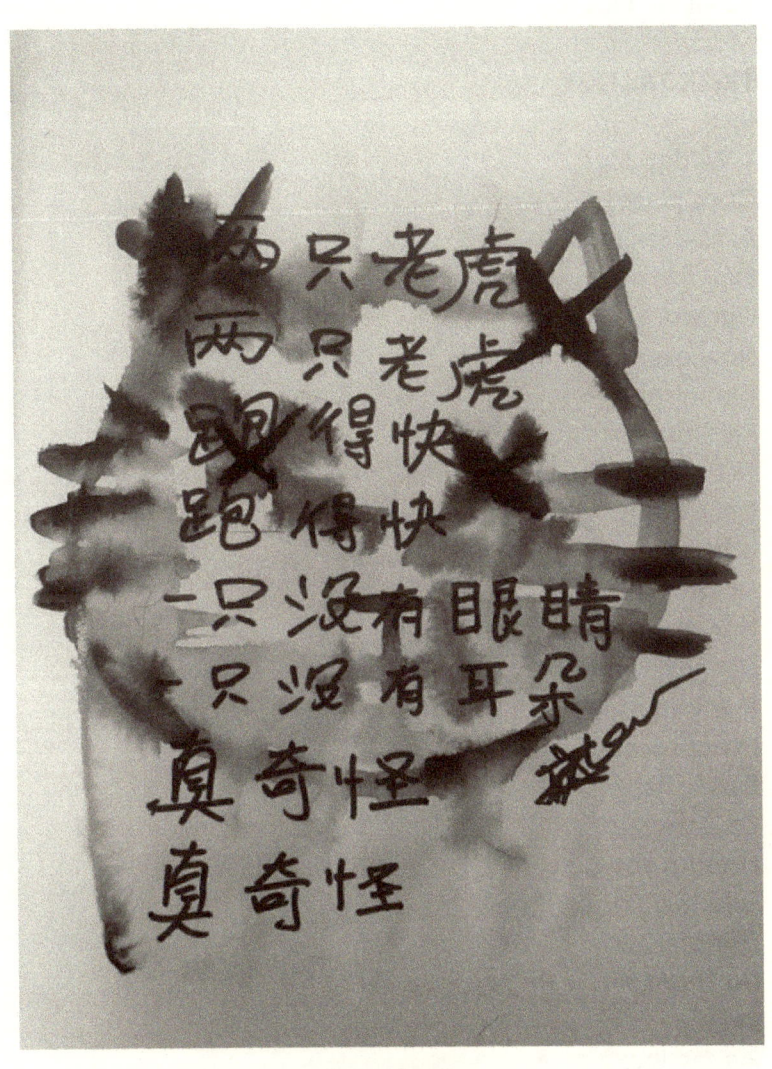

Two Tigers
Kemlyn Tan Bappe
Watercolor and Ink
2021

KEMLYN TAN BAPPE

TIGER TRILOGY

I. Wild spaces
Once places
Across spanned
Expanse over
Our world
Now ever shrinking
Diminishing
Rainforests
Oceans
Once teeming
With an array
Of life
Now the extinct
List grows exponentially
In my short lifetime
Other species
Barely hang
On a thread
I mourn you:
Splendid Poison Frog
Spit Macaw
Northern White Rhinoceros
Baiji
Pyrean Ibex
Western Black Rhinoceros
The Passenger Pigeon
The Quagga
Our recent casualties
Resulting from
Sins of human commission and omission
Lord, we have failed you

As stewards of Eden
I am the worst of all
For it is from the barrels of my ancestor's gun
That claimed the life of
Singapore's last tiger

> *Notes
> My great-great uncle, Tan Tian Quee was a part of the hunting party that shot the last tiger in Singapore.
> http://2ndshot.blogspot.com/2010/10/2nd-shot-last-tiger-of-singapore.html?

II. Top Ten Reasons Why You Shouldn't Pull The Trigger
1. Hey, I didn't eat them. It was my cousin twice removed.
2. It's rather unsportsmanlike. I was napping by Choa Chu Kang Road.
3. Coolies? Impossible, they are not my cup of tea. Pompous Englishm…...muffins. Hmmm, I am definitely vegetarian.
4. I am adorable. Look at these big, cute cat eyes.
5. Do you really want to go down in history as the one who killed off the last tiger?
6. Shouldn't we follow the diplomatic process?
7. Surely, you wouldn't shoot an unarmed man.
8. I have connections with renowned poets. My friend knows William Blake?
9. Let's bring in an interpreter. You clearly do not grasp tiger or our culture.
10. If man cannot live by bread alone, how can a tiger do the same?

III. I am the Man
I was man enough
Enough to pull the trigger
Triggering future hate poems in generations to come
Come be reasonable
Reasons reasons reasons
I needed a tiger pelt rug with glass eyes
Eyes now staring at me through nightmares
Nights filled with new full arousal
Roused with essence brewed from tiger's paw and dried
                                                      penises
It is all for posterity
For progeny
For populating our country
It was worth it
I am worth it
I am the man
I am the man
I am the man

VIRGINIA BARRETT

PHASES

I

If we asked the stars unsteady light
what they are saying
would we hear foreboding
or accept that more is seen while sleeping
how perceptive when we close our eyes
day brings too much glare
the rain so many voices
speaking all at once as it falls
gathering encounters
we are driven to wreck with heavy steps
the moon wipes clean.

II

We have cut down the most precious trees
fires for warmth burning us
or we shiver here in our own shadows
stretched long or short before us
the streets laid with enormous stones
we carried from far away places
our backs bent under the weight
under the night sky
pushing us to draw new star-charts
tied to fresh myths
eyes fixed on changing phases.

JUDITH AYN BERNHARD

THE RAIN IN SPAIN

the rain in Spain may
fall mainly on the plain

but in California now

it feels like it's never
going to rain again

here the air is as dry
as Ebenezer's eye and

the bone weary wind

will return once again
to heat up our dreams

soon an ugly orange
haze will fill up the air

as smoke from wild fires

invades our lives through
our clothes and our hair

do we have to stop living
in far away forests or sit

and wait for rising waters
to devour and destroy us

or can we work together
to change things around

and fix the planet from
the skies to the ground

SCOTT BIRD

LOOK AT THIS ZENITH

apex of sun across night north
there is a ruby-throated hummingbird
in every single star
and a star in every honeysuckle
and the nectar and stamens fill dank
spaces along Africa's East coast with black fields
of rhino hiding rot bereft of ivory

every tower will now bow down to fossil
every sea to rise and recede
reseeding those buffalo plains
on this little blue drop of Tatanake
and we will raise corn in the old-fashioned way
in the highways and byways all vinecovered
over village upon terraced village

spread out like mycelium veils
devouring oil slicks and old tires of
abstract wealth, and in exchange potatoes
that grow madly along the banks
of asparagus and I too will arise and become
a freshwater Lake but free of this competitive
modernity, who clears whole fields of solar power

and damns ancient rivers to electrify hydrogen
and who scrambles to gag first before the
Sun goes down the long red horizon
before post Cambrian wanes
and ages wave out
their sorrowed hands
to a new Moon so clear in love and full

CHARLES CURTIS BLACKWELL

CLIMATE CHANGE MAN MADE DISASTERS

Climate Change Man Made Disasters
And Lowndes County Alabama
(Catherine Coleman Flowers
A Worrier)

Ice cap melting/Islands disappearing
Photochemical smog/Drought
Forest fires/Cellophane madness/Oil spills
Acid rain/Mud slides/Health epidemics
Lowndes County sewage
Raw sewage, spilling over everywhere
Backyards Front Streets
Sewage in the water, in the air
Catherine demanding
To clean this shit up
Tons on top of tons of shit
For it turned Lowndes county
      Into a shithole county
           And soon and very soon
                America will be a shithole

DAN BRADY

LONG AFTER TIME WHAT IS?

Long, long from now
When all that is now is forgotten
More than simply buried in the mind
Or the earth
More than simply covered up
But gone
Truly dissolved through the immense passages of time
During which the Earth has completely reformed its surface
And is done turning under its continents
When every human thing has vanished
Beyond all hope of ever being found
When no living thing recalls our peculiar smell or fear
And life has recovered all that was lost.

When all that is now
Is absolutely gone
Beyond anyone's knowledge of what once was
Is or might yet be –

Long after time
When there is no forgiving
Or forgetting
When the quiet world simply rests
Through its long horizons
And the moon casts down innocent light
Where winds are gentle
And the forests have come back into their own
Long after
Long, long after all that we've dreamt of
When even the greatest of our myriad possessions
Have been broken down into the smallest of grains
And so have become part and parcel to the earth
And each is simply moved by the wind   or the water
And all has been absorbed by

And recycled millions of times
Through plants and animals
The living carpet that life is upon this world

When there is no evidence of any kind
When matter is so purified
Until purity is no longer a relative term
And all is well.

Long after time   has gone
When it is no longer a measure
When measuring is no longer needful
When counting is as forgotten as numbers
And sense is a term applied
Only to the eyes, ears, tongue, nose or touch.

Long after time   what is?

What will be?

When peace itself is the only thing
And nature is let to do what it does best
After the recycling of all that we once were
Has erased all the details
Leveled the playing field
Once and for all

Long after
Long, long after time
What is the chance
That the Earth will decide to try once more
To weave spirit into matter
Manifesting such illumination
As brings consciousness into life
And if not in human form...
Then certainly with a prayer that this time
Its promise will be kept!

DANIEL BROOKS

FOR MY PEOPLE (LOVE WILL BRING US BACK TOGETHER)

I do it for you I do it for me
I do it for the people
Until we're free

I do it for millions of ancestors
And living things
We'll never find in the ocean
Buried beneath roads
Buildings and walking feet
I do it for the people under
The watchful eye of the state

I do it for you I do it for me
I do it for the people
Until we're free

I do it for African brothers
And sisters living in my heart
Fighting to unite the continent
I do it for freedom fighters
And freedom lovers who crushed
What needed to be crushed
And buried what needed
To be buried

I do it for you I do it for me
I do it for the people
Until we're free

KRISTINA BROWN

BOOM
dedicated to the people of Ukraine who resist invasion as I write

Boom boom   boom boom   boom
The heat is on.
            The planet is hot
                       and growing hotter.
Forests burn and glaciers crack.
Everywhere
All over the world
         we hear the sound   of marching boots
And of lies.
Boom boom   boom boom
Rivers run dry.
But the words of strong men

Wannabe tyrants   dictators
                     and entrepreneurs flow,
Feed anger, paranoia, and hatred
                 for their power, profit, and
perverse pleasure.
Oceans rise.
The tyrants and wannabe dictators
                 talk violence and law and order,
chaos and control,
        crime and punishment.
They paint refugees and desperate immigrants as prone to violence,

Spin delusions   of difference and separation
Of language and race, and racial purity

Of superior blood, whether Anglo Saxon or Slavic or Han Chinese.

Boom boom   boom boom

Crops fail and deserts spread
Tyrants talk
Of the untrustworthy others,
Whoever they are,
        whoever the dictator needs them to be:
People who aren't the right color
Don't practice the right religion
              speak the right language
Think the right thoughts,
Whatever the tyrant or dictator to be says those are.

Boom boom   boom boom

Storms kill ancient trees,
              scour hillsides of every living thing.
Prisons fill.
Reeducation camps
          Detention camps   pop up all over
from China to Italy
        from the US to Brazil.
Maybe
    not death camps
Maybe
    not places of mass murder
                  yet.
But dangerous places where many people die.

Boom boom   boom boom

Recording every move
                       every glance
                                         the blink of an eye in real
time,
The technology of surveillance,
manipulation by machine and algorithm,
makes close control of minds and bodies cheap and easy.
Boom boom   boom boom

Putin invades Ukraine,
                waits until after the Genocide Olympics
   as a courtesy to Xi.
Lies proliferate.
                Killers and liars rule.
Wars rage.

Wars that pretend to be about religion or language,
but provide the pretext
                   for ripping off resources
            like Ukrainian wheat fields and rare metals.
   World War
              isn't here yet.
Not yet.

But the rhetoric of race
                religion
                       national identity   heats up.
        And so does the planet.

Boom boom boom

JEREMY CANTOR

END OF THE ANTHROPOCENE

The evolution of our skills outpaced
the evolution of our judgement, so

here we are employing those collective
skills by leaping head-first from the cliff's edge

all together (nearly all together —
some did not come freely to the edge

and needed to be pushed or pulled or shackled
to each other or to us or both),

accelerating toward the rocks below
(at rates we have the skills to calculate),

placing bets (with odds we have the skills
to calculate) on who will live the longest.

YOLANDA CATZALCO

ESTO, DIFÍCIL DE ESCRIBIR

Esto, difícil de traducir, escribir.
Que ha sucedido con la sociedad
De América? De San Francisco,
En los Estados Unidos.

Un hombre sin vivienda, desamparado
Durmiendo en su saco de dormir,
Alguien lo quemó
Mientras dormía en su bolsa de dormir
Un viernes por la mañana
El 8 de octubre. El siguiente martes, murió.

Aún más deficil de comprender
Murió en las calles 25 y South Van Ness
Dos cuadras y medio de donde vivo.

Una calle de distancia de donde
Un carro me atropelló
En la calle 26 y S. Van Ness
El lunes, el 13 de septiembre
Entre las 8 y las 8:15 de la mañana
Cuando yo caminaba de una esquina
A la otra esquina
En la misma calle, con la luz verde.

Yo le hecho la culpa
Al aparato estatal nacional, etc.
Por sus posiciones en contra
En contra de los desamparados, los pobres.

Es difícil caminar entre tanto
Dolor en el corazón, tragedía, y fascismo.

YOLANDA CATZALCO

THIS HARD TO WRITE POEM

This, hard to translate, to write.
What has become of society?
Of America? Of San Francisco,
In the United States.

A homeless man, defenseless
Sleeping in his sleeping bag
Somebody burned him
Asleep in his sleeping bag
On Friday morning,
the 8 of October.
He died the following Tuesday.

Even harder to come to grips,
It happened on 25th and South Van Ness,
Two blocks and a half from where I live.

A block away from where
I was struck by a car
On 26th and S. Van Ness,
Monday morning, September 13,
Between 8 and 8:15 am
When I was walking
halfway on the crosswalk
with a green light.

I blame
The state apparatus and the capitalist class
For the anti homeless, anti-poor
hysteria/propaganda.

It's hard, walking amidst so much
Heartache, tragedy, and fascism.

Pero, tenemos que luchar
Contra la propaganda fascista, corporativa
Luchar con el conocimiento
Que el futuro está en nuestras manos.

Escriban, lean, aboguen
Defendiendo el derecho de
Los pobres, los sin techo, los desamparados
A la vida.
No podemos continuar como especies si no.

Exigimos que los/las representantes
Gubernamentales elegidos a todos niveles
Alojan a los desamparados.

Yet, we have to counter
The fascist propaganda
Fight with the knowledge
That the future is up to us.

Write, read, speak, advocate
Defend the right of
The poor, the unhoused, the defenseless
To life.
We can't continue as a species otherwise.

DEMAND the Government
Elected officials at all levels,
House the Homeless!!!

(Translated from Spanish by the author)

MARCO CINQUE *(Italy)*

SCUSATE

Scusate se siamo fuggiti
dalle guerre che voi nutrite
con le vostre stesse armi

Scusate se ci siamo avvelenati
con i rifiuti tossici sotterrati
dalle vostre potenti industrie

Scusate se avete dissanguato
la nostra terra, deprivandoci
di ogni possibile risorsa

Scusate la nostra povertà
figlia della vostra ricchezza
dei vostri neo-colonialismi

Scusate se veniamo massacrati
e disturbiamo le vostre vacanze
col nostro sangue invisibile

Scusate se occupiamo
coi nostri sudici corpi
i vostri centri di detenzione

Scusate se ci spezziamo la schiena
nei vostri campi di pomodoro
schiavi senza alcun diritto

Scusate se viviamo nelle
vostre baracche di lamiera
ammucchiati come bestie

MARCO CINQUE *(Italy)*

EXCUSE US

Excuse us for fleeing
the wars that you fed
with your own arms

Excuse us for getting poisoned
with the toxic waste buried
by your powerful industries

Excuse us if you've bled
out our land, depriving us
of any possible resource

Excuse our poverty
daughter of your richness
of your neo-colonialisms

Excuse us for being massacred
and for disturbing your vacation
with our invisible blood

Excuse us for occupying
your detention centers
with our filthy bodies

Excuse us for breaking our
backs in your tomato fields
slaves without any right

Excuse us for living in
your tin huts
stacked like beasts

Scusate per la nostra presenza
che causa ogni vostra crisi
e non vi fa vivere bene

Scusate se le vostre leggi
non sono abbastanza severe
e molti di voi vorrebbero la forca

Scusate se esistiamo
se respiriamo, se mangiamo
persino se osiamo sognare

Scusate se non siamo morti in mare
e se invece lo siamo, scusate ancora
l'impudenza d'avervelo fatto sapere.

Excuse us for our presence
that causes each of your crises
and doesn't make you live well

Excuse us if your laws
aren't strict enough
and many of you would love the gallows

Excuse us for existing,
for breathing, for eating
even for daring to dream

Excuse us if we didn't die at sea
and if we did, excuse us again
the impudence of informing you.

(Translated from Italian by Alessandra Bava)

Agneta Falk

BOBBY COLEMAN

THE LAST POET SALUTES THE LAST FLOWER

Many generations loved thee, sweet blossom
your surprise appearances, your vulnerability
drooping at a season's end

such poignant departures
and joyous returns

but now, without bees, unloved
there will be no more of you

no more seers, nor seen,
nor memory of your scent

there was a chance before which was ignored
by my former self now human-machine,
part repulsive rocket in space

(I have devices learning
to hug me back you know —
the problem is they also learned
how to swipe what they hug of my dough)

See how I have already forgotten thee,
last flower; I am the dying voice
of the last distracted poet

so I must apologize, wee beauty,
for dragging your total
innocence into my suicide

FRANCIS COMBES *(France)*

LE POETE EST UN COMMUNISTE

Tout poète — même s'il l'ignore
et même s'il le refuse —
tout poète est un communiste.
Tout poète
partout et toujours
dit que le monde,
la terre et les mers,
les arbres, les oiseaux, les villes
et tout ce qu'elles contiennent,
même les palais, les Champs-Élysées,
les ponts sur la Seine,
le sourire des femmes
(même celles qui ne sont pas la tienne...
Mais en vérité, aucune n'est ta propriété)
et le sourire des enfants
et celui des hommes
et le regard des bêtes
tout,
la Terre entière,
le monde et ses saisons,
l'automne et ses richesses,
l'hiver et ses plaisirs,
le printemps, ses promesses,
l'été et ses moissons,
tout est à nous.
Tout ce que nous ne possédons pas,
par les pouvoirs que nous confèrent
l'imagination, la poésie
et le rêve nécessaire
de l'humanité

FRANCIS COMBES *(France)*

THE POET IS A COMMUNIST

Every poet — even if he doesn't know it
and even if he denies it —
every poet is a communist.
Every poet
always and everywhere
says that the world
the earth and the oceans,
the trees, the birds, the cities
and all they include
even the palais, the Champs-Élysées,
the bridges on the Seine,
the smiles of women
(even those who are not yours . . .
Though truly, no one belongs to you)
and the smiles of children
and those of men
and the looks of the animals
everything
the entire Earth
the world and its seasons
autumn and its riches
winter and its pleasures
spring, its promises
summer and its harvests
everything is ours.
Everything we don't have,
by the powers that give us
imagination, poetry
and the vital dream
of humanity,

tout nous appartient
et nous appartenons à tout.
Toute la vie sur Terre est notre affaire.
Tout nous parle et nous répondons de tout.
Tout est à nous
et partout et toujours
tout
nous est à partager.

(In « *Lettres d'amour, poste restante* », 2020)

everything belongs to us
and we belong to everything.
All life on Earth is our business.
Everything speaks to us and we respond to everything.
Everything is ours
and always and everywhere
everything
is for us to share.

(Translated from French by Barbara Paschke)

KITTY COSTELLO

BLINDSPOTS

Where we do not want to look
is a tomb we must jump into
a well we must throw ourselves down
with no guarantee of ever hitting water

Pitiful small hands try to push blood
back into heads that are bleeding onto the street
try to push bullets
back into barrels of guns

Not a single voice cries out
as everyone walks the wrong road together
just for the company—
a shifting of bones within skins

The pillows are fluffed up too large
the heads propped away from the bodies
No one monitors the dream world
Some are caught sleeping on their feet

The world fills with synthetic dirt
with plastic aquarium plants
The eyes of fishes swell
Birds unscrew themselves from the sky

And still we walk upright as if everywhere
legs had not been lost to landmines
In bed we somehow still reach
our lips out for kisses

Some eyes break, won't blink
Those few go sane, rise fiercely from the sheets
step straight to the edge of the volcano
and witness the fire
                    without falling in.

J. VERN CROMARTIE

AFTER KATRINA IN THE CRESCENT CITY

Katrina came with howling winds
breaking levees with rushing water
pouring down Canal Street

Katrina came to the Crescent City
blasting away at brick and mortar
blasting away at bone and sinew
blasting away at hope and promise

on the left coast
we saw televised images
of Katrina hitting the Big Easy
on the chin with a knockout punch
and wondered whether
it could come back
from all that

on the left coast
we wondered where is Bush
we wondered what will Bush do
we wondered what can Bush do

was he sitting there
in Crawford, Texas
paralyzed by low poll numbers
as desperate people in a devastated city
struggled along without water
struggled along without food
struggled along without shelter

Pops Armstrong once said

do you know what it means
to miss New Orleans

i rest assured
with a ray of hope
that the ancient city
of Pops Armstrong
will return to glory

i rest assured
with a ray of hope
that the ancient city
of Marie Laveau
will return to glory

i rest assured
with a ray of hope
that the ancient city
of Congo Square
will return to glory
like
a
Benu.

Author's note:
This poem was written on August 31, 2005.

ANITA CRUZ

The OLD RIVER

The old river leaves for a destination.
It carries even the last boat lost in directions.
It is made of water from blood of the dead.
It surged to end of earth with water hyacinths.

It woke up the rivers of the moon
even as the whimsical rock kept her distance
more antiseptic than iodine or chlorine.
To confirm that it touches this river of fainting men.

The exhaustion of the earth flows down from
the melting polar poles that melted in torrents
to the ripped cupboards of hills and valleys
and carcasses of trees that guarded us from landslides.

The moon will die as the sun glares in earnest even
as they never know the exact time when darkness
will cover us on toxic atmosphere of carbon & lead
to confirm that the earth has lost its orbit to nowhere.

ROMEO ALCALA CRUZ

FACE LOST IN RIVER WILDERNESS

Do not fill postcards in memories of my life
on earth between my heart and the luxury
of passion that stretches a river trying to
touch the hungry mouth of the ocean after
the tides tried to whip and lash and hold me
accountable to safeguard, protect the waters
from being poisoned from the runoff of my
discontent. The horrors of my defeat after
I sickened the towns, cities and countries of
my wanton greed and excess development.
This I called progress which are other words
for: I, Me and Myself to exclude the fishes
that still swim in my dreams.

No! Don't ask me if I still remember where and
how I picked the white shells off Efren Enverga
of fish mills and pesticides as I slide down to
the river that complains of my depredations as it
dies of slow death after the houses drain its sewage
at its crystal waters to shoo the fishes away as the
stain of progress kills everybody and drags us to the abyss
down below. It is hateful to remember when the ghosts
of the night appear as I hugged the water hyacinths, telling
them not to drift away. But my demise is guaranteed
as darkness has slain the moon as it plunges to the
sea. I dripped sweat in my sleep like a faucet that
refuses to be shut tight. In the mirror of my heart,
I cannot find shelter as the climate has pushed the
dark clouds of rain away, like a leper. Only the disguised
face of Lamon Bay is a lovely face to see, though a
mutilated one above the ruffling waves.

How did the world revolve this way? My earth was young and easy going. Did it want to grow old in haste, as it tried to amass as much wealth as it can in the shortest time as possible? In the dead of the night, as the moon retreated from the highest peak, I can still see her hand reach out for me after the waters receded away in the low tide, enticed like magic to expose the skeletons of dead fishes embedded in the rocks.

I hallucinated: Open my heart to the dream of the night when I followed the river like an eel without sight, obeying its soothing currents like daughter to her mother. The climate beast was taunting me for my confession of the crime as winds of misfortune howled from four corners of the earth. He tried to warn me about my impending demise as the moon plunges noiselessly to the sea.

JOHN CURL

SHE SAID / HE SAID

Don't worry about trying to fix it, he said,
we've destroyed this world past
redemption, beyond habitability, it's dead,
murdered, our task now is to leave and colonize
another planet. Wow. He really said that.
Seriously. He imagines heroically saving
humanity from extinction by escaping to some
spacesuit utopia in the stars. That is the
Puritan's eye, escaping the corrupt Old World,
reinventing yourself in a new city on a hill in
an imagined tabula rasa, the eye of the imperialist,
dreaming that there is always some new
pristine place to start over again and plunder,
even now when people have pillaged the entire
earth and there is no place left here to plunder.

Then go, if you must, she said,
to your own suicide, but
don't expect me to buy you that spaceship.

Even if life really did come here
long ago from the stars, she said, and
even if that means we are star people too,
even so, we have been here so long we
are now and forever earth people, and
this earth does not belong to us;
we belong to her. This planet is not
an object we can use, abuse, discard like
so much garbage. Our task now is
not to escape but to stay right here, to
hold fast to earth, to learn to live here,
to protect her. We are now and forever
inseparable from her, our wild watery habitat,
our precious green mother.

AMIT DAHIYABADSHAH *(India)*

NILGIRI MOUNTAINS

Nilgiri mountains, vast, eternal
blue bossomed maternal.
We have come to adore
the essence of all that was before.

Prodigals can't see so we must seek with tired minds and
                                            eyes grown weak
the milk of life flow over your breast in shola stream and
glade and nest

Somewhere in here lies an umblical cord
cut by wire word and sword

Over twenty millenia or so ago
as we stole and fled from nature's door

Now the seed of time and grain is spent
with a harvest of thorn the land is rent
to seek forgiveness two thieves return
our sins go on but still we yearn

to raise an offering of sweat
to the height of a hill
to touch a high mountain meadow
with the greening of will

to taste a sundancing stream
with the thirst of ages
to pick a small perfect flower
and read it like pages

to offer warm breath
to a cold morning star
to take one perfect moment
and not stretch it too far.

CAROL DENNY

INTERNET SENSATION

a poet sent me lyrics
through the internet
I pressed my printer button
and they came
they blew out of the printer
like a hard wind
and I taped them to the phone poles
with his name

the night moved aside and said
so serious
are you sure you want to drink
it all the way
and I said it's so simple
just come with me
and the night walked right beside me
until day

now all the poles in town
are speaking poetry
they think that's what it is
and so do I
everybody's walking backwards
trying to read it all
trying to dance around the poles
and trying to fly

I love it when they ask
are you serious
there's nothing that makes me
laugh so hard

GERMAIN DROOGENBROODT *(BELGIUM)*

THE ROAD

Where did you come from
where will you go?

How long will last
your eternity

–planet?

Reversible is everything
but where lies the verge

who knows about the reversal
the darkening
the night?

Time is pressing, pushing the sand

Scratch the word
in the stone and hope
that it remains

–not

as testament.

From "The Road" (Tao)

CARLOS RAÚL DUFFLAR

ONE MUST HAVE JUSTICE TO GIVE JUSTICE
(May The Truth Of Leonard Peltier Set Him Free)

It is dawn that rises in the light to our planet
Songs of joy from the heart of Mother Earth
The moon, the sky, the stars, the air,
the plants, the animals, the fish
food to feed the people
And now the signs of stormy weather lying ahead
The floods, the fire rising
Polluting the water, air pollution,
the rising tides of sea level
global warming, poison affecting people's lives
Let us join together in a circle of the lies, the madness,
and the vast silence
For the victory over the greedy
To save our environment
The Earth is our planet
And the rulers of the Earth are not man but Earth
To stop mass destruction
He who lives not in harmony will fade like the wind
On this sunny Autumn afternoon,
I follow my footprints, to Ashuwillticook Stream,
Cliffs and valleys along the Mohegan-Mohawk Trails
While the raven flies above
I have made a pilgrimage to Spirit Mountain
And sitting on top and listening to
Richie Havens singing
"Here comes the Sun and it's alright"
Remembering an old friend and sage
Chief Falling Wind
Marching for justice to inherit
the freedom of our Earth

with the Martin Luther King
Poor People's Campaign of 1968
Marching down the streets of Washington, DC
And rallying at the Supreme Court
for Mother Earth, compassion, love, and understanding

MARIA J. ESTRADA

MAYBE

There's plastic in my sushi
    Maybe
There's lead in the water
    Most Likely
There's Mad Cow in my steak
    Probably
There's cancer in the air
    No Doubt

Before abundant fish are dead
Before fresh water evaporates
Before pastoral cows kill *us*
Before hot air disintegrates young skin

Maybe—

Our minds will expand beyond the edges of infinity
And you, free from the yoke of social media pings
And constant consumerist lies
Free from this dying system

Maybe—
    You will make
        The earth, and you, and me
        Whole.

AGNETA FALK

COLD WHERE IT SHOULD BE WARM

The wind out there is banging around
bending everything furiously in its way
the weather like people are on the move
it's warm where it should be cold
wet where it should be dry, and snow's
piling up in places that never saw snow

but unlike these people, storms have names:
Carla, Dora, Frederic, Hattie, Hortense,
Ivan, Joan, Stan, Roxanne, Klaus
and the formidable, Katrina, 2005

it took 25 years to tear down the Berlin wall
now pieces of that wall hang in deafening silence
in museums around the world.

no one knows the face of this war, as it
glides over the accelerating landscape
crushing everything in its way
the roads and the sea's full of fleeing people

and who is fighting whom, and who is who
and where to, and why did it happen there
and not here, and should I lock my door now

before it's too late, but isn't it already too late?
somebody's got a foot in my door, and my door's
no longer my door

and no matter how many new walls go up
people will keep on coming, nothing can
stop fear from moving to safer land

and nothing's safer than keeping
your door open to those who are
on the wrong side of a border
whose only hope is your out-stretched arms.

MAURO FFORTISSIMO

THE LABORIOUS WAY OF BEING

Takes work to make nest,
brittle branches, high winds, rains
the dosage of our galaxy
little things I've learned
enough with the puncture of the planet!
put things back where they belong
no plastic in the oceans
no pig's shit into rivers
no oil on beaches and corals

The laborious way of being
looking at the night sky
not to see Elon's satellites
but far stars, some already dead
others telescoped nearer to us
and you and I so close at night
feeling the weight of your breasts
and my testicles like the crows
crowing unhappily perched on a brittle branch
when the wind approaches
nah it won't be us...
we are Ipanema
we are Venice
all carnival together...

The laborious way of being
ends when the fire is lit
when the wave crashes
let it be known
we were once here
in total awe

and then we began to inquire
the more we learned, we realized,
the less we knew
and kept going...
salt water to quench a thirst...

MARK FISHBEIN

U.N. RESOLUTION 3452

We cannot begin to consider the end of war until
we cease all forms of torture and rape.

The wolves bite off chunks of a body
In their cages of stone and metal-
The tortured abandon hope to pain,
Their flesh defiled in drift to death.

On every continent,
Tribe against tribe,
God against god,
The army against the people,
The primal male infesting woman.

The nations have signed the dotted line
Condemn, condemn, condemn
What no mind can comprehend.

Statistics only count the surrendered,
Those left numb forever.
Somewhere, this instant,
In the abundance of all suffering creatures,
A bound victim confronts its spider-
Sadism clings to hate in echoing chambers
As a human beast screams in disbelief
       The cruelty of the wolf.

MARCOS DE SOUSA FREITAS *(Brazil)*

OLHE PARA CIMA E EM TODAS AS DIREÇÕES
        ao artista plástico e ativista ambiental indonésio
                      Tisna Sanjaya

i. citarum river
os peixes poluídos do rio Citarum dividem espaços
e oxigênio da água com as pilhas de garrafas de plásticos.
crianças em saltos plásticos mergulham no meio dos
                                    plásticos.
crianças em barcos de alumínio catam, para venda,
latas de alumínios e plásticos.
os peixes poluídos do rio Citarum dividem espaços
e oxigênio da água com as pilhas de garrafas de plásticos.
nas margens e nos pilares de pontes agarram-se
enxurradas de plásticos coloridos, galhos, vasilhames,
carcaças de bois, sofás.
campos de arroz contaminados. turbilhões de líquidos
despejados de fábricas têxteis.
os peixes poluídos do rio Citarum dividem espaços
e oxigênio da água com as pilhas de garrafas de plásticos.
quantos outros rios - mundo a fora - são também rios de
                                      plásticos?

ii. lagoas marginais do rio Poty
os aguapés e os sapos não moram mais nas lagoas
os aguapés e os sapos não moram mais nas lagoas
essas quedam soterradas exatamente onde ergueram-se
luxuosos shopping centers e ventilados apartamentos
com varandas amplas, de onde pode-se contemplar
o majestoso pôr do sol, o resplandecente tapete verde de
                                      aguapés
sempre bem alimentado pelos esgotos não tratados
os aguapés e os sapos não moram mais nas lagoas
os aguapés e os sapos não moram mais nas lagoas

MARCOS DE SOUSA FREITAS *(Brazil)*

LOOK UP AND IN ALL DIRECTIONS
    to indonesian plastic artist and environmental activist
                                         Tisna Sanjaya

i. Citarum river
the Citarum river polluted fishes share spaces
and oxygen from water with stacks of plastic bottles.
children in plastic jump dive among the plastics.
children in aluminum boats collect aluminum cans
and plastics for sale.
the Citarum river polluted fishes share spaces
and oxygen from water with stacks of plastic bottles.
on the banks and on the pillars of bridges floods cling
colorful plastics, twigs, containers, ox carcasses,
                                            sofas.
contaminated rice fields. whirls of liquids poured from
textile factories.
the Citarum river polluted fishes share spaces
and oxygen from water with stacks of plastic bottles.
how many other rivers - around the world - are also plastic
                                            rivers?

ii. Poty river marginal ponds
water hyacinths and frogs no longer live in ponds
water hyacinths and frogs no longer live in ponds
they fall buried exactly where they rose
luxurious shopping malls and ventilated apartments
with large balconies, from where you can contemplate
the majestic sunset, the resplendent green carpet of water
                                            hyacinth
  always well fed by untreated sewage
water hyacinths and frogs no longer live in ponds
water hyacinths and frogs no longer live in ponds

iii. conversa de louco ritmada pelo bater das asas de borboletas azuis
solitário udu faz ninho na barranca do rio da cerca
tendo chuva, somente 0,8% de água será absorvida
o pato mergulhão ainda vive na floresta de cabeça para
                                                    baixo
o cerrado tem papel central na distribuição das águas
a celulose de florestas plantadas gera papel para o noticiário e novos livros
os corais do Pacífico estão perdendo a cor rapidamente
a anchova é prejudicada pelo aumento da temperatura do
                                                                        mar
efeito estufa desertificação degelo aerossóis
cantos de cigarras anunciam as chuvas vindouras
urso polar é encontrado, com fome, a 800 km de seu
                                                   habitat natural
no xingu cacique tenta manter viva a língua walapiti
no chão as folhas secas do outono são pisadas por tênis de palmilhas
                recicladas
                            a partir de plásticos marinhos

iv. enquadramento de um novo dia
por mais que a gente tente
o mundo continuará a girar
por mais que a gente o represe
o rio sempre chegará ao mar

iii. crazy talk rhythmed by the beating of blue butterfly wings
a solitary amazonian motmot makes his nest on the bank of the cerca river
if it rains, only 0.8% of the water will be absorbed
the brazilian merganser still lives in the so-called upside-
down forest
the savanna has a central role in the distribution of water
pulp from planted forests generates newspaper and new
books
pacific corals are rapidly losing color
anchovy is harmed by rising sea temperature
greenhouse effect desertification thaw aerosols
cicadas' chants herald the coming rains
polar bear is found, hungry, 800 km from its natural
habitat
in the xingu chief tries to keep the walapiti language alive
on the ground dry autumn leaves are trampled by sneakers with
recycled
marine plastics soles

iv. framing a new day
no matter how hard we try
the world will keep on turning
no matter how much we dam it
the river will always reach the sea

(Translated from Portuguese by the author)

RAFAEL JESÚS GONZÁLEZ

LA LLAMADA

¿Qué puedo decir para incitarte
    a defender la Tierra?
¿Recordarte como se siente el sol?
¿el sabor de la sal, el olor del laurel?
¿El chirrido de grillo en noche de verano,
el arco iris después de lluvia?
        ¿Lo que es amar?
¿Imploraré a tu goce
    o a tu pavor?
Puede ser terrible la Tierra
en sus tormentas y en sus temblores
pero es la medida de cual paraíso
    imaginemos jamás.
Tú y yo moriremos demasiado pronto
    pero que no siga la vida
        es más allá de aceptable.
¿Qué puedo decir para que ames la vida
suficiente para que actúes y alces la voz
    en su defensa?

RAFAEL JESÚS GONZÁLEZ

THE CALL

What can I say to entice you
      to defend the Earth?
Remind you how the sun feels?
The taste of salt, the smell of bay?
a cricket's chirp on a summer night,
the rainbow after rain?
           What it is to love?
Shall I appeal to your joy
      or to your fear?
Earth can be terrible
in her storms & in her quakes
but she is the measure of any paradise
      we will ever imagine.
You & I will die all too soon
      but that life will not go on
           is beyond accepting.
What can I say to make you love life
enough to act & raise your voice
           in its defense?

ART GOODTIMES

COVID WINTER SOLSTICE: THE GREAT CONJUNCTION
for Tony & Crow

Got to see itki big eye-lensed
at Danny's Fruita observatory
Hay bales eight feet high
smeared with mud. Hand shaped
Rounding one's way around & into
a central viewing courtyard
to block out surface photon static

The rings of Saturn & moons of
Jupiter side by side in the Great Conjunction
The heavens coming together
Even as we go on pulling ourselves apart
The gravity of our discontents
stronger than all our shared histories

Yes we will wobble, Capt. Barefoot agrees
We will blur, but let's hope we work ourselves
out of this experiment we call civilization
Homo koyaanisqatsi
Ours an infectious template adapting
as we are to Earth's every niche & peak

May we resume
a reciprocal place in the Chthulucene pantheon
Even as our immediate cosmos appears
about to go spinning back into
some illusory Anthropocene normal
As if human *techne* alone ruled
on this galactic battleground of the Milky Way

Shaking hands, unmasked. Hugging again
As if our kin were sovereign planets
somehow protected in the Goldilocks Zone
of the stars we are

Unaware of the unseen viral black holes
coming to gobble our overflow

*NOTA BENE:
"Ki" is a grammatical neologism Indigenous science writer Robin Wall Kimmerer advocates using in place of "it", "its", "it's" or "itself" to help correct English's objectification of the world. As a pre-school teacher I learned that we learn by going through the known to the unknown. So instead of substituting "ki", I've chosen to add the Indigenous neologism to our neutral English pronoun as a suffix, changing the way we speak of things in English from inanimate to animate, "itki." The neologist term is harvested from the last syllable of a longer word in Potawatomi for an "earth being." That syllable, "ki", is itself a Bodéwadmimwen suffix meaning "from the living earth."

EGON GÜNTHER *(Germany)*

FORTGESETZTER LANDRAUB

> *... the wasted buffalo killed for sport*
> *true universes in their globed eyes*
> *—Charles Plymell*

   entseelte natur
gestutzt von menschenhand
  greift raum
  entblößt das land
von alten wilden geistern
    nomaden & lemuren
  vergrault bestellten bodens feinde
  treibt sie aus dem fest mit gier um-
    gürteten gebiet
   ins äußerste
über den regenbogenrand
  herab
in die garstige erzählung
versehrter stimmen mörderischer qual
  die dem süßen walten
   sich wandelnder wildnis wiederkehr
    in den fesseln der zeit
      ein bitteres ende weist

SAG EINMAL
wer sorgt sich schon
  um das geschlecht der sterne
        im weltall
wenn der olymp verwaist ist
  aber bewahrt aller schrecken
        der unterwelt

EGON GÜNTHER *(Germany)*

LANDGRABBING CONTINUED
>*... the wasted buffalo killed for sport*
>*true universes in their globed eyes*
>—Charles Plymell

      soulless nature
pruned by man's hand
      gaining ground
      laying bare the land
of ancient savage spirits
      nomads & lemurs
      scaring foes of tilled soil
      expelling them where greed
      firmly rules
      into *finis Terrae*
      beyond and below the rainbow
      margin
      to enter the nasty tale
of voices hurt by murderous pain
    which for the sweet reign
      of changing wilderness re-emergent
      in the fetters of time
        points out a bitter ending

C'MON TELL ME
devil who cares about
      the gender of stars
           in the universe
once mount Olympus is orphaned
      while keeping all horrors
           of the underworld

(Translated from German by Jörg W. Rademacher)

JACK HIRSCHMAN

THE HOUSE OF THE SETTING SUN

"Become a rag again and the poorest may wave you"
                Pier Paolo Pasolini: To the Red Flag

I put my mouth to your misery, New Orleans,
inundated and soaking with death.
Here lies: war lies piled so high, this floating
prison of a cemetery cries out of rage
at the end of its breath. Here, in the last delta,
Desire lies on its side, is rolled, and rolled
over upon by its own government, and crushed.

Summertime is over and the livin' is dead,
and 'round midnight all hopes are looted.
No one will come clean of the Katrina
of New Orleans in this sinking
house of the setting sun.
Bodies so Black and so blue from loving
what wouldn't spit on their shoes if they
needed a shine. Let alone a dime. Or water.

America, you were always scorched earth
in our mouths, always a baptism of crap,
always a rain of disaster streaming
down the panes of our broken eyes.
Now our rags are the most torn,
our jazz the most blue, our poor the poorest
that can be worn in the soul's thrift-shop.
Now that all is lost and there's only nothing
to lose... "Long live the courage
and the sorrow and the innocence of the poor!"
The real flag's in tatters. Begin to wave it.

EVERETT HOAGLAND

VENOMOUS CONSTRICTOR

Every 4 to 8 years, it needs to seem changed.

And the venomous, standing, right-to-
left-swaying, split tongue, lie-spitting

serpent that always aims for our eyes
gets down, rubs up against a jagged truth

about it and slides out of itself seemingly
renewed, with a glistening red, white and blue

beauty that has been, is always only on its scales.
And the body of alluring abstractions, the coiling,

suffocating isms it is snake forward into the future
until it swells so from all it has swallowed whole,

yet again, it is pressured to shed its skin.

ANTONELLA IASCHI *(Italy)*

FUOCO

In ogni parte del mondo
l'orizzonte si allontana dai diritti
e l'umanità consuma le sue ore
in miserie economiche e mentali.

Simboli minacciosi tornano nelle piazze
siedono nelle stanze dei bottoni
e governano nel nome delle banche
a favore di pochi carnefici.

Anche la malattia diventa un lusso
se hai soldi ti salvi, oppure muori
mentre salgono in borsa le quote
di chi dovrebbe garantire le cure.

Le caste e l'ignoranza lottano
rivolgendo le armi al più povero
senza accorgersi dei fili guidati
dai burattinai della storia.

Fuoco davanti e fuoco dietro
nella tempesta di un futuro incerto
che vuole i popoli relegati on line
perché è delle piazze la lotta.

Ci raccontano che il mondo è fermo
intrappolato nella pandemia
mentre le guerre e la fame continuano
ad arricchire i soliti noti.

L'unica strada che possiamo percorrere
è quella del passato che ci univa
Se la bandiera rossa adesso è straccio
con lei ci fasceremo le ferite.

ANTONELLA IASCHI *(Italy)*

FIRE

In every part of the world
the horizon moves away from rights
and humanity spends its hours
in economic and mental misery.

Menacing symbols return in the squares,
sitting in the war rooms,
governing in the name of the banks
in favour of a few executioners.

Even illness becomes a luxury
if you have money you are saved, otherwise you die
while the shares climb in the stock market
of those that should guarantee the cure.

The castes and ignorance fight
turning armaments toward the poorer
not noticing the strings guided
by the historic puppeteers.

Fire in front and fire in back
in the storm of an uncertain future
that wants the populace relegated online
because the struggle is in the piazzas.

They say the world is stationary
trapped in the pandemic
while war and famine continue
to enrich the usual ones.

The only road that we can follow
is that of the past which united us:
if the red flag is now like a rag
with it we can bandage our wounds.

(Translated from Italian by Danilo Koren)

BRUCE ISAACSON

FROM THE ARTIST'S STUDIO

In her studio, the painted bear is bigger
than good or evil or any
televised tap dance at truth. Now,
the top of the world is a snow cone—
a chunk of shaved ice dripping
sweet, chocolaty
minerals to ships below.
A vision both
beautiful & savage as
a murder mystery where the corpse
is laid out on a banquet table.
The painted bear looks at us
calmly but
without understanding.
Finally, we understand.
Finally, the hand of God is seen as
the hand of Man—
a narcissus, an obsessive itch
we can't scratch. The end time
is not atom bomb, not
genetic mutation.
It is knowledge
turned to power
turned to madness.
God hath given us dominion.
We know we are important—
Look! We are on television!
We are the show that is
canceling itself,
mutant cells eating the host.
We're the alpha, the omega, the

be-all and End.
Nature was better than a garden.
Bears were not good or evil—
they were ferocious
and magnificent.
There is no place left for bears.
We roar like bears at
one another instead.
The new prophesy to justify
the ways of Man to God?
Do what thou wilt—
the modern prophet said
and so people have.
Sometimes the artists catch a flash—
a little glint of something more
and try to get it on television
next to stock footage of
polar bears floating
stranded on ice.

ZIBA KARBASSI (Iran)

شعری از زیبا کرباسی

انتهای بی انتهاست
و از اعماق تاریک سر دانشمند جوانی سنگی پرتاب می‌شود و
زمین تکه پاره
پاره
تکه پاره
مثل صدا که حرف را پاره می‌کند
در دهان وزبان
تا شعر شود

کتف‌های زمین را از دو سو بسته اند و
بوزینه‌ها هورتمه کشان و
لی لی کنان
از این سو به آن سوی خواب می‌پرند

زانوان زمین ترک برمی دارد
شانوانش جر می‌خورد
هق هق از گریه پریده
شانه‌هایش کو
قاه قاه از خنده می‌پرد
شانه‌هایش کو

پرنده‌های بی پر و پرواز روییده اند از میان هق هق وترک
ای به درک

بگذارید آسمان ستاره‌هایش را تف کند بر صورتتان
ای به درک

بگذارید آفتاب روی برگرداندتان
ای به درک

که کوه‌ها عق بزنند بر سر و پیکرتان
ای به درک

ZIBA KARBASSI *(Iran)*

TO HELL WITH IT

The end of no ending
And from the inmost ache of the brain of a young inventor
                          a stone jerks free
And the earth breaks up
in tiny pieces
tiny tiny pieces
as a voice shattering in its semiotic stricture
must in the mouth of language –
become a poem!

And the shoulders of earth tighten in trauma
And the tree-monkeys hopscotch from this to that side of the
                                                   dream

flying

The knees of the earth splinter
The shoulders are cracked apart
The ss-ss-sso of sob is snapped off from sobbing, and where
                                 are the shudders ?
The voice of hh-hhha's hurled apart from laughter, and
                                 where are the shivers ?
And wingless flightless birds are flocked between the cracks
                                                       and
              the voices of weeping.

To hell with it !
Let the sky spit its stars on your face

To hell with it !
Let the sun turn its heat from you

ای به درک کبکان سر در برف ای به درک

رها کنید زمین این زن جر خورده را
رها
فرو بگذار یدش
مادرتان را گاییده اید ای بی پدران
ادیپان بی فردا

آغوش بودم اگر
آغوش بودم اگر
آغوش بودم های می‌فشردمش تا تیمار
آغوش بودم اگر

To hell with it !

And the mountains vomit intestines over you
To hell with it !

To hell with it you bird hurled in the snow for hiding

To hell with it !

Leave this earth, this ripped-open woman, leave her,
you-mother-fucker : you-oedipus-of-no-
                              future

If I were a hug
If I were a hu-hug,
If I were a hug I would hold this wrapped
                              so tightly O

Until all of it healed over …. If I
were a hug …

(Translated from Farsi by Stephen Watts
and Ziba Karbassi)

ELLIOT KATZ

THINKING ABOUT EMPTINESS FROM NORTH AMERICA'S SKULL

>"*With no obstruction,*
>*How can there be*
>*Absence of obstruction?*"
>   Nagarjuna, *Verses from the Center*,
>   tr. Stephen Bachelor

Over the horizon bright
jagged bolts of white lightning
are thrown like javelins
from the top of the continent.

Where are they landing?
Nowhere.
Who is throwing those electrified spears?
No one.

Outside the cabin window after the storm
the tops of some of the mountain's evergreen trees
have become a dirty orange
as if they were ever orange trees.

I wonder what natural processes
or acts of industry
have turned the tops of these trees orange?
Is industry a part of nature's course?

From the edge of the mountain
I see dozens of oil rigs dot the landscape
Even three or four years ago
I could only see one or two.

What license from the galaxy
could give oil & gas companies the right
to despoil Canada's boreal forest?
Could a business contract give this right?

Who will stop the logging industry's
ever-widening clear-cuts?
Is it possible that trees exploit us
like this in another universe?

At 11 pm, the sun has gone down
and the treetops look green again
What kept me from seeing what was there?
What in this cabin window creates illusion?

With record-breaking heat, the fire lookouts
are on "extreme hazard" all week
They are calling smoke locations into the radio
all day & through the night.

Are there really other humans listening
at another end of the radio?
Who heard Vivian call in that smoky ridge?
If she didn't see it, would someone else?

On the FM radio, I listen to local gossip.
No war talk. The disaster in Iraq must be
over up here! For global warming, the locals
know it's past the tipping point.

At midnight, it finally gets dark
Soon all appearances will vanish
Goodnight Vivian, goodnight Eliot
With luck we'll all meet again in the morning.

D.L. LANG

IN THE NAME OF PROFIT THE EARTH BURNS

On the news we watch them go to space,
searching for planets on which to escape,
burning up fuel at exorbitant rates
as if there were no holes in the ozone layer.

Capitalists encourage endless growth
except when it comes to human welfare.
They sell us lies and sow division
just so they can keep a high dividend.

Their lips preach democracy and freedom,
yet no one is free under the yoke of greed.
They force us all to live in austerity
when we have the resources for prosperity.

They do not build products to last,
so many objects wind up in the trash.
They use this planet like a dumpster
and deny the human consequences.

They dump pollutants into our rivers
and then sell what's left to us in a bottle.
They make toxic the very air we breathe
just to make some new tchotchkes.

They buy up companies and patents
that could provide us with solutions
just to shut down all production
so they can maintain their profits.

They steal resources from across the world,

ensuring that other nations remain poor.
They avoid providing for all humankind
while building bombs and starting wars.

They care more about their bank accounts
than any of their next-door neighbors.
While they feed their endless greed,
so many folks cannot meet basic needs,
people are dying from preventable disease,
and children lie homeless in the streets.

While the earth burns the capitalists hoard,
not caring about the struggling masses.
Such chaos they sow in the name of profit!
It's about time we did something to stop it!

So many problems could be solved
if we put aside earth's exploitation
to rebuild this and every nation
to serve its people with compassion.

We can build a brand-new world
where the needs of all humanity are met
instead of succumbing to these fascists
who mindlessly destroy our only planet.

We must act now before it's too late!
We will have a world without greed and hate!

ANN LEONARD

MISSION ST FIRE

from La Panaderia's dusty windows,
just off mission,
I gazed at the the crater—
the charred timbers/twisted metal remains
 extracted—
now just a deep socket
where the 1907 wedding cake hotel had
gone up
in a four-alarm fire—
flames leaping and ripping
exploding out windows—
woodwork and glass hurled to the ground

and I remembered the Las Vulnerablēs—
the trio of women
I'd seen everyday near the hotel doors—
broken   fragile   surviving—
the small spark within still gleaming—
their sole blessing
a roof over their heads
in the worn-out hotel—

the three vulnerables—
living embodiments
of the Fates' spoken words—
the unfolding of tragedy
on america's mean streets—
awash with hard poverty

and I remembered Rosamunde
thrown from a window by a man in a meth rage—

now with her walker/wearing a slip—
a frail wraith on the streets—
barefoot and begging—
holding out her hand—
"help me, I'm hungry!"
the toothless chanting ringing out—
Rosamunde, beseeching again and again,
"help me please! help me!"

and, I'd last seen laughing Alba from a passing bus—
how she'd loved to dance and drink—
but now she lay
with her long hair in the gutter—
her legs spread in the street—
blacked out where any car could crush her—
 she was dressed in peasant ruffles—
  —it was Carnaval week—

and I'd heard Deniece at the mercado,
just before the fire—
her eyes wide as she whispered,
"the cops they found friend Keisha—
in the alley by the hotel,
 with a spike in one arm—
  and a fresh gash in the other—
and you know what that means…"
 she stepped back—
"but, don't you worry about me, now—
I ain't goin' Nowhere—
 cuz, I've had my day in the sun
  and I can Remember—
no, I ain't ready to check out yet…"

Rosamunde, Alba, Deniece—
their home, the hotel,

burnt to the ground—
  where are they now, and the dozens of others?
are they living in tents, or in boxes?
  or asleep in a culvert out at the beach?

"the Las Vulnerablēs, where are they?"
I'll stand up and ask
  the developers, the landlords—
  the politicians who
crown themselves kings—
  the Fates of our century—
spinning the tragedy, measuring the portions—
men who make themselves rich at the expense of the poor—
  "our most vulnerable—I'm asking—
    where are they now—
      what will you do?"

GENNY LIM

AFTER THE RAIN

Can we not see beauty till we let go our hold of it?
-Rabindranath Tagore

The Sun descended on the land
A spark fell, alighting broom brush and sugar pine
The forest ignited like a moth in flames
Evergreens crackled, rooftops crashed
Men beat back flames under burning
Sequoias slumped like amputees
The wail and cries of bears, coyotes, horses and deer
echoed over four million acres, over 10,000 homes
Only chimneys left standing, stairs leading nowhere
Paradise buried in ashes

Those who hadn't left were trapped
Exhausted, homeless, emptied of care or blame
Far from birds and flocks and old memories
Would the next architect resurrect from the
empty grave a replica of what once was?
The fugitives pray for rain to extinguish
the last embers of attachment so that nature
might reveal herself as the Goddess of Mercy
before the next strike of the match

After the Camp Fire, the Cal Fire, Inyo Creek
SCU, August, LNU Lightning, Thomas, Rattlesnake
Interstate 5, North Complex, Bend, Carr, Zaca and Pass
The Crews, Soledad, Mineral, Coyote, Hog, Gold
July, Blue Jay, Red Salmon, Brandy, Apple, Pond
North, Stagecoach, Wolf, Lake, Ranch, Hills, Loyalton
Beaver River, Dome, CZU lightning, Willow, Peak and

Lava fires, the rats scattered

Memories, plans, passports, dreams, Last Will and
Testaments, old and new growth, gone up in smoke
in what's become an annual ritual sacrifice

A melody drifts into the fog as we look up
at the scarred yet consoling starry night
Yeah, life isn't all it's cracked up to be
But love in the aftermath of loss will grace
the first buds of purple sky lupine poking their heads
from earth with tiny sprouts of Aspens reaching for light

MARK LIPMAN

> *She was born innocent enough,*
> *eighteenth down the list ...*

CASSANDRA
(also known as Hurricane Sandy)

Tropical
  depression
 an improbable
      left turn
Dangerous transformation
        Waters warmer than normal
                Growing effect of the global
            The worst of nature
              combined as one
            red flag warnings
           high altitude jet stream
            surging waves
            skeptics aware too late.
Low lying lands give way
   to the funneled mass of nature
  concentrated onto the weakest points
        Screams for help
           as they pull the plug
              submerging the city into darkness
            explosions and sweeping fires
                light the sky in red and orange
               ships thrown ashore
            homes tumbled over
   and the poor, as always
     swept away and forgotten.

ANGELINA LLONGUERAS *(Catalonia)*

FUGIDA

Se us vaig escapar.

Vaig ser llesta i vaig marxar.

No ho podia aguantar més.

No hi hauria cap després.

Me'n vaig anar.

Em vaig acostumar

a no fer-vos cas,

no donar un mal pas.

Em vaig alliberar

a un preu ben car.

Em vaig desarrelar,

vaig deixar anar

vaig desaprendre a estimar.

Vaig fugir sense pensar.

Barcelona, gener de 2022

ANGELINA LLONGUERAS (*Catalonia*)

ESCAPE

I escaped from you.

I was clever and I left.

I couldn't stand it any longer.

There wouldn't be any afterwards.

I went away.

I got used to

to not pay attention to you,

to not take a bad step.

I got free

at a high price.

I uprooted myself

I let it go

I unlearned to love.

I escaped without a thought.

Barcelona, January 2022

(Translated from Catalan by the author)

OSCAR LOCATELLI *(Italy)*

UN BRUTTO VOLO

Un pettirosso
ha varcato i confini
della nostra mente;
la nostra mente... piena
di filo spinato,
annodata come un nido
abbandonato.

Quel pettirosso
è qui davanti a me:
non trova più acqua,
il suo canto è incerto,
le sue piume annerite
hanno un unico colore.

Il pettirosso
ha sorvolato chilometri
di umanità:
pochi centimetri
di dignità.

OSCAR LOCATELLI *(Italy)*

A BAD FLIGHT

A robin
has crossed the boundaries
of our mind;
our mind... full
of barbed wire,
knotted like an abandoned
nest.

That robin
is here in front of me:
it can no longer find water,
its song is uncertain,
its blackened feathers
have only one color.

The robin
has flown over kilometers
of humanity:
a few centimeters
of dignity.

(Translated from Italian by the author)

ANNA LOMBARDO *(Italy)*

NON RIESCO A RESPIRARE

sotto queste ginocchia che
molestano l'aria

Non posso ridere
sotto questo sinistro cielo droni
cambiano le mie nuvole in bombe

Nessuno ascolta
il fremito delle foglie
delle foreste ridotte ad aridi campi

E la madre terra è sopraffatta
e le pance di molti ancora vuote
lungo strade e vicoli

E troppi cadaveri
galleggiano sopra quel
mare rosso vino

E molti altri cadono da impalcature
e altri ancora restano
in fila per una briciola di pane

Perché tu, e tu, e tu
imperial-capital-fascist-misogenista
sei ancora avido e presente

Non riesco a respirare
ma io lo voglio, adesso
ne ho bisogno

ANNA LOMBARDO *(Italy)*

I CANNOT BREATHE

under their knees that
harass the air

I can't laugh
under this sinister sky
drones change my clouds into bombs

Nobody listens
the trembling of the leaves
of the forests reduced to arid fields

And mother earth is overwhelmed
and the bellies of many still empty
along streets and alleys

And too many corpses
float above that
red wine sea

And many others fall from scaffolding
and still others remain
lined up for a crumb of bread

Because you, and you, and you
imperial-capital-fascist-misogynist
you are still greedy and present

I cannot breathe
but I want it now
I need it

Sorelle e fratelli
mostriamo loro quanto
lungo e profumato sia il nostro respiro

Lasciamo che esso indichi la strada
e, come nuovo Mosè,
apra sentieri

Verso quest'altra aria nuova
più giovane e fresca.

Sisters and brothers
let's show them how much
may our breath be long and fragrant

Let it lead the way
and, like new Moses,
open paths

Towards this other new air
younger and fresher.

(Translated from Italian by the author)

KIRK LUMPKIN

DOWN TO THE CROSSROADS
    I went down to the crossroads, fell down on my knees.
    —Robert Johnson (from the blues song "Crossroads")

On each side of the center stripe
    of the winding night road
    matching orange reflectors rise
    just above the asphalt's black
    and each pair of these reflectors
    tonight are watching me
    with the burning eyes of ghost alligators
    whose bodies are hidden beneath the surface
    of this dark twisting river of oil.
And we are <u>not</u> riding
    on the moaning black snake of voodoo,
    this is <u>not</u> the vehicle to carry us
        to cosmic connection—
    the wind wailing,
    the engines mechanically drumming
    and I feel us going faster and faster down
    leaving behind
        the collateral roadkill
        of wild and native extinction,
    rolling down cancer alley,
    down toward the crossroads of reckoning
    where whichever way we turn
        leads to a dead end
    or takes us squarely back
        to where we came from,
    caught in the karma of car culture
    we can't drive our way out of this box,
    we've sold ourselves into the slavery of addiction,
    and possessed by corporations

      we're accelerating downhill toward disaster
      seemingly unable to even imagine
           life without driving,
             life without buzzing with the power of
                        internal combustion,
      and the whole planet is being sucked into this
                    smoking undercurrent
      while the devil rides shotgun
           humming to himself thinking
           he's got a deed guaranteeing
           he can keep on mining
           our collective soul for his power.

But there is a counter movement in the shadow world
      and the spirits of our ancestors
           are coming back to re-claim their remains,
      and there will be consequences
           for the graves we've robbed,
           for not having let
           our fossil ancestors
           rest in peace,
           instead forcing them into a hellish zombie
                        after-life
           to fuel our craving for machines to do our
                        bidding,
      they are coming back to collect the unpaid tolls
           for all that we have run over
           and all that we have paved,
      to teach us some respect,
      and to help us find our way.

And here at the crossroads
      doesn't have to be
      where our minds and bodies
           go separate ways,

  where our love is crucified
  and where we pawn our souls for energy—
We can stop here,
  turn the engine and headlights off,
  get out of our cars.
  —stretch
    & breathe—

let go of the weight we're carrying,
walk away from the madness,
open ourselves
  to the beauty of the night sky,
  to the life of the world,
  to synchronicity,
offer ourselves
  to love, to the gods,
  to the wild future
  still evolving on this sacred ground of
         graves,

kneel and touch the Earth

and we're home.

JUAN ALCALA LUNA

BEYOND FORGETTING

Beyond forgetting as every living thing has a right
to fresh air, as every plant has a right to flower,

as any type of grass for land & birds for varied colors
sizes. Thus any bird can eat seeds, alight on a tree,
sing a song to welcome Spring even moan the falling
of rain. The song of my nightingale on this damp Spring

day is a pleasing one, after a long rainbow and during
the arrival of a mail truck with letters from my daughters
who sent Valentine cards: descriptions of their lives
where they found countries that love self-driving electric
cars, houses that open and close to the light of the sun.
That they love to walk through parks bigger than NY's

Central Park or SFO's Golden Gate Park. The public
                                                                   libraries
posted posters of endangered fishes on the walls. How to
conserve rainwater in huge containers attached to their
houses as appendages. I hush and pat my dog on the
back as he runs on the ragged field outside knowing the
world has given its lungs to us to breathe in freedom,

count the petals of roses, even chant a song of a bird.

BIPLAB MAJEE বিপ্লব মাজী *(India)*

স্বপ্নের বাগানগুলি

আমাদের স্বপ্নের বাগানগুলি
        একে একে পুড়ে ছাই,
ভস্মাধার হাতে নিয়ে আমরা হতাশ!
কেউ ভাবছি তত্ত্বে ভুল
           কেউ ভাবছি প্রয়োগে--
সমুদ্র সূর্য নিয়ে সরে গেছে দূরে,
আর আমরা হলুদ দীর্ঘশ্বাসে ভাবছি,
  --এ আমরা কোথায় এলাম?
আকাশে শঙ্খচিল নেই কেন?
আমরা আবার কোথা থেকে শুরু করব?
কে দেখাবে পথ?
       ছাইভস্ম থেকে ফিনিক্সের মতো
কবে আবার জেগে উঠবে স্বপ্নের বাগানগুলি?
যেখানে মাথা রেখে শান্তিতে ঘুমোব.....

২৪ জুলাই ২০১৮ সকাল

BIPLAB MAJEE *(India)*

DREAM GARDENS

Our dream gardens are being burnt
                one after another
We are depressed with the urn in our hands
While one thinks the theory is wrong
the other thinks that the
                application is wrong.
Taking the sun along with the sea
goes afar
And we are thinking with the yellow sighs
Where do we reach?
       Why there is no seagull in the sky?
Where shall we start again?
       Who will show us the path?
When will the dream gardens come
     out like a phoenix bird from the ashes
Where we sleep in peace...

(Translated from Bengali by Nandita Bhattacharya)

devorah major

UWA: HUMAN FREE

have you ever sat alone
hilltop eyeing a vast cloudless sky
a wedge of gulls parting the blue

would it be
less without you
or would serenity
still reign

have you leaned against a redwood
inside their family circle
and heard thick moss hum
the sweetness of green
filling your mouth
as the musk of rotting leaves
tickles your nose
and the birds quiet again
with your stillness

would it be less
without you
or remain one of terra's
ancient temples

have you been held
by the ocean's fingertips
salt gems soothing skin
kelp swaying beneath your belly
wave rhythms drumming the shore

and wondered if

it would be less
without you or
remain the womb
of eternal creation

how tragic would it
really be if humanity
was no longer earth's
primary predator
because gaea cleansed her skin

of we who devour
the eden she has provided

uwa- igbo for earth

AHCENE MARICHE *(Algeria)*

LA TOILE D'ARAIGNÉE

Devant une toile d'araignée
A méditer et à l'observer
Je me suis laissé
A elle bien tendue,
Je m'imagine suspendu,
M'en libérer est peine perdue.

Ce que mes yeux voient
Éveille mon émoi
Et me pousse à réfléchir.
Profondément angoissé
Occupé par ma pensée
Comment m'en sortir ?

Une mouche vient tournoyer
Autour de la toile, tout près
De l'araignée aux aguets.
Fatiguée, elle s'y est posée
Aussitôt elle est happée
En une minute sucée

Que de mouches ont ainsi péri
Et moi je réfléchi
Au pourquoi de ceci.
Enfin je comprends
Que l'araignée les attend
Pour en vivre s'entend

Arrive un grand taon
Tout en bourdonnant
Fort et bien portant
La toile est secouée
D'un seul coup transpercée
L'hyménoptère est passé

AHCENE MARICHE *(Algeria)*

THE SPIDERWEB

In front of a spider's web
To meditate and observe
I am left
Caught in it
I imagine myself suspended,
To free myself is wasted effort.

What my eyes see
Awakens my excitement
And makes me think.
Deeply distressed
Occupied with my thoughts
How do I escape?

A fly comes circling
Around the web, very close
To the spider on the lookout.
Tired, she landed there
Quickly she was caught
In a minute sucked in.

So many flies have thus perished
And me, I reflect
Why this is.
Finally I understand
That the spider is waiting for them
To live off them, of course

Comes a big gadfly
All buzzing
Strong and healthy
The web is shaken
Suddenly pierced
The wasp has passed through

La toile n'est que silhouette
Elle ne gêne ni n'inquiète
Il le fait de belle lurette
C'est pour cela qu'il s'en passe
Car le plus fort passe
Et le plus faible trépasse

Ainsi sont les lois
Telles des toiles je les vois
Le faible s'y débat
C'est un perdu combat
Le plus fort ne s'y fait pas
Il n'en fait pas cas

A une toile d'araignée
Je compare les lois
Elle prend la mouche facilement
Mais pas le bourdon
Par sa force, il la perfore
A ce propos nous sommes d'accord

Les lois profitent tout le temps
A ceux qui sont nantis
Ceux qui les subissent souvent
Sont les plus démunis
Médite ! Toi le sage, toi le savant
Pour qui sont-elles tissées ?

The web is only a silhouette
It doesn't bother or worry
It does this for a long time
This is why it happens
Because the strongest pass through
And the weakest pass away

So the laws are
Like webs as I see them
The weak struggle
It's a lost fight
The strongest don't get done like that
It doesn't matter

To a spider's web
I compare the laws
It picks up the fly easily
But not the bumblebee
By his strength, he breaks through
On this we agree

Laws always profit
The wealthy
Those who suffer from them often
Are the poorest
Meditate! You the wise, you the scholar
For whom are they woven?

(Translated from French by John Curl)

Roger Strobel

ÁNGEL L. MARTÍNEZ

A 'MEMORY OF PLAGUE(S)
(Mother Earth Revival)

I remember in the plague's early days
when all the jets vanished from the sky
not a droning to be heard
(if you're on the airport path
you know what I mean)
I remember the whirring trucks went silent too
more diesel for free bus rides
something I had to see with my eyes I tell you
I tell this because amid all gloom
there, that little hope
even when it's hard to breathe
by smog sky
or under death squad boots
or in hospitals that close and never open
by word of the profits
we have to fight
we don't need normal
we need Mother Earth
renewed
for our new day

ALBERTO MASALA *(Italy)*

A MAHMOUD DARWISH

noi che amiamo le case
dove con scrupolo accurato
abbiamo congelato smisurate
e inservibili cataste di memoria

noi che amiamo le strade
che facciamo uscendo dalle case
i soliti percorsi familiari
confortanti e sicuri

noi
che possiamo tornare senza fretta
e tornando vediamo
tutte le nostre case illuminate
aspettarci al silenzio di ogni sera

noi che abbiamo famiglia
che torniamo in famiglia
assistendo alle liti di famiglia
e mangiamo in feste di famiglia
e andiamo ai funerali e ai matrimoni

noi con le nostre regole
con le nostre certezze accumulate
come monumentali verità
e con le nostalgie e le commozioni
e le infinite possibilità

noi
che moriamo in letti d'ospedale
con i segni di croce e le cure adeguate
che la guerra è un disagio del momento
alla televisione e ne soffriamo
poi c'è l'altra notizia

ALBERTO MASALA *(Italy)*

TO MAHMOUD DARWISH

we who love houses
where with scrupulous care
we have frozen huge
and useless memory stacks

we who love the roads
we walk by leaving the houses
the usual comforting and safe
familiar paths

we
who can return without haste
and while returning we see
all our illuminated houses
waiting for us in the silence of every evening

we who have family
we who go back to the family
witnessing family quarrels
and we eat in family celebrations
and we go to funerals and weddings

we with our rules
with our accumulated certainties
as monumental truths
and with nostalgia and emotion
and the infinite possibilities

we
who die in hospital beds
with the signs of the cross and proper cares
that war is an inconvenience of the moment
on television and we suffer from it
then there's the other news

noi
che non ne abbiamo colpa
se c'è un mare di mezzo
se siamo nati qui
e qui siamo rimasti
se di là è tutto più infelice
e non c'è acqua o luce
e nemmeno parole
se la logica già
scrive questa realtà
con regolarità crudele
se quella rabbia è sempre sorvegliata
dall'oggettività dei fatti
che chiamiamo destino

noi
che abbiamo le parole
sempre troppo in ritardo
e anche le bocche per cantare
l'evidenza alla quale
non avremmo voluto appartenere

noi
che scriviamo libri accumulando
e a quale prezzo
e poi scrivendo il vuoto
dei nostri passi incerti
intorno alle parole della farsa

noi
potremmo amare una casa che non c'è?
Una casa crollata? L'incertezza?
Sapremmo dare un titolo all'assenza?
All'esilio? alla fame? alla rovina?

we
who are not guilty
if there is a sea in between
if we were born here
and here we remained
and in there it's all more unhappy
and there is no water nor light
and not even words
if logic already
writes this reality
with cruel regularity
if that anger is always surveilled
by the objectivity of the facts
that we call fate

we
that we have the words
always too late
and also mouths for singing
the obvious to which
we would not have wanted to belong

we
who write books accumulating
at what price
and then writing the void
of our uncertain steps
circling around the words of farce

we
could we love a house that is not there?
A collapsed house? The uncertainty?
Could we give a title to absence?
To exile? To hunger? To ruin?

E intanto quelle voci
quelle voci
e intanto quelle voci nel cervello
in un unico canto...

Mahmoud... lo chiedo a te...
Ma è così che si scrive un genocidio?

And meanwhile those voices
those voices
and meanwhile those voices in the brain
together in one singing ...

Mahmoud ... I ask you ...
Is this the way a genocide is written down?

(Translated from Italian by the author)

TOMMI AVICOLLI MECCA

JUNK ON THE MOON

they left trash among its
ancient craters
almost half a million pounds
containers with the excrement
the piss of astronauts
and several American flags
now tattered and faded
even a bible in an
abandoned rover
they left footprints
permanently frozen into
the lifeless soil of
this oversized rock
this bastard child
ripped from its womb
without warning
billions of years ago
an inspiration to poets
and dreamers
a friend to the loners
and the drifters
it plays tug of war
with the oceans
hide and seek
with the clouds
it won't be long before
it's colonized
mined
its green cheese surface
cut into slices thick and thin
conquered or sold or stolen
stripped of everything
of value
just like the earth

KAREN MELANDER-MAGOON

METHANE AND TEARS

Now bubbling up in shallow lakes
Or Puget Sound
Bubbling from seismic plates
Overrich in nutrition
Undernourished in oxygen
Overnourished in algae
Bubbling up from melting ice
Once solid Arctic masses
Melting frozen earth
Centuries old natural gas
Methane endangering our air
Eutrophy of our planet
Smothering away life
Smothering away oxygen
Gradually asphyxiating
Our world
The ocean cries for you
The rivers and their tributaries
Weep into your soul
The stars sing to you
Dropping slowly into the night ocean
As drops extinguish their song
The moon crowns you with its light
Wrapping you in song and sorrow
Flowing from its heart of music and weeping
Rising in the night
Sinking slowly against the damp dawn
Pulling tides of tears

SARAH MENEFEE

THE SEASON I LONG FOR
   (a suite of earthy meditations)

my young friends
step out to caress the world
into necessary geometries

'cosmic utopia' he said

*

how many different
fish deities

do you think there
have been?

*

will there be rain
this strange year

to soak the homeless
overtaken by its puddles?

the season I long for
is also heartless
(per human arrangement)

*

in the belly
of the beast

Jonah lays his
meager feast

*

'we should be
gamboling and playing

on this planet
all our lives' he said

*

the cast-off
have the wings
of forbidden sleep

they flap
thru your dreams

the age's
dearest angels

*

asking for nothing
but the deep dignity
of giving

a drop to the stream
of starry evolution

TUREEDA MIKELL

BREAKING BREAD BURDEN

In the early 90s, at the Center for African and
African American Arts & Culture, an 84-year-old
African American W.W.II vet, husband, father,
thin, tall, frail, and weary eyed shares his experience
coming home after the ended, on a train headed home
after the war.

We were proud young Black men
We fought died risked life and limbs
Defending this Country
In the name of freedom
For U.S. of A, front lines
We protect our country against Nazis
America said,
Committed crimes against humanity
We see Nazis like kkk...a Mississippi god damn

We see Jews suffer what we suffer by kkk
Accept endure another killing method

We thought **if** we had defeated this enemy
 If we could prove ourselves
   Good American soldiers
    Fight for American ideals
     Pledge allegiance to this flag's
      One nation under their god
       We'd be seen as equals
There'd be no difference between us
  and White Americans

When we got news the war was over

Blood bowel flesh blown stench
Still stuck in the hairs of our nose,
We went from battlefields to barracks
Clean up and wait for the buses
To take us to the train station

Black, Whites, Colored, all cheering
Shouting, crying, shell shocked and
Segregated
Wait
Pay it no never mind
Just want to get on that train
Sit down to a hot meal and
Go home to what's left of our families

We're alive, we survived

Train whistle blows
Slows to a stop
Steam heat bellows beneath its belly
Stirring the cool air… ghost like
Trying to warn us of something

Military guards signal us to board
We Black-coloreds help one another
War behind us, hungry
We walk toward the dining car
When out of nowhere
A large white U.S. soldier blocks our path
Stops us in our tracks
Legs spread
Bayonet in hand
Orders us to, **stand down.**
Tells us,
"Disobey my order and

you'll be court marshaled."

Tell us, "Find a seat.
   The kitchen will bring food to you "

We lose our appetite
Look at one another
Numb from mind trauma again
We ask ourselves over and over

Why in god's name did this happen?

We were proud soldiers
Lost life, family, eyes, and limbs
to defend this Country"
But this country still could not
Break bread with us?

Hours pass
Train makes another stop
Picks up several troops of captured Nazis
Guess they were hungrier because they
marched them passed us
  into the dinning car
   like we weren't even there

Like we were the enemy
Like we caused the holocaust
Like we experimented on Jews
  Without anesthesia
   Branded them like cattle
    Gassed millions in ovens
     Placed hundreds in front of firing squads
       Dumping them in mass graves

Fed them Nazis in the dining car
   In spite of the U.S. government telling us
      Nazis had committed crimes against humanity
         And needed to be stopped

They Broke bread with them……
   but not with us
Fed them Nazis hot food, and
   Made us wait outside the dining car
      For cold sandwiches

What did we fight for?
We killed for America
Lost life, family, eyes and limbs
   to defend America

Do White Americans serve other whites
   No matter how vile they act?

What is this man's story?

Elder vet water swollen eyes
   Rolls tides into mine
     Noting

The War didn't end
   It moved!

GAIL MITCHELL

CHENEDU VALENTINE OKOBI
For The Okobi Family

There could be no piecemeal
way of saying what it feels like
to know the sister of one
whose brother was tased out of his life?
7 times, for menacing act of walking.

Her Facebook post said
"I have always been afraid to get the call"...
Just the thought of it
Makes me shudder inside

That violence fueled by blind vision fear and ignorance
Has finally hit home

Hate reckless abandon
lies and corruption are on stage
Masquerading as the law

How do these officers of the law?
Manage to kiss their Mother's cheek
and not remember
They took a son's life.

How do these officers of the law?
Compartmentalize death

Walking while Black should not be Lethal

EDWARD MYCUE

A GREAT FINAL MUSIC

That words dream motion

makes life glorious

puts raw silk to silence

gives music tongue,

reveals in all the rainbow colors

how nature comes listening

to seed bursting,

to the prairie garnet and

desert chimney peridot,

leaving the wind behind.

Actions matter.

Thoughts matter.

All flow into

a great final music.

MAJID NAFICY

WILDFIRE

This house has two windows
And I, like a migrant,
Move between them
To escape the burning sun.

In the morning, I sit at the northern window
And repair poetry
With my talking computer.
In the evening, I go to the southern window
Sit on my rocking chair
And listen to my talking book.

But today, the air has fever
Like a swollen body,*
The sun is an ugly wound*
Opening its mouth
And the house smells of smoke.

A fire has caught the skirt of the city.
Right now, hundreds of firefighters
Are engaging with the wildfire
In groves, canyons and towns,
And thousands of homeless men, women and children
Have moved to shelters
With their horses, dogs and cats.

I wish it would rain.
Then I could sit
At this window sometimes
And sometimes at the other one
And listen to the sound of the rain
Falling equally over houses,
Both burned and unburned.

* From "It Is Night,",a poem written by the Iranian poet Nima Yushij.
* From "Prose of Trans-Siberian," a poem written by the Swiss poet
                                                        Blaise Cendrars.
"And yet it does turn!" Galileo Galilei (1564-1642)

BILL NEVINS

FIRE-WALL

"A brief parting from those dear/Is the worst man has to fear."
                      --William Yeats, "Under Ben Bulben"

Flames broke the ridge line just the other day,
A day like any other day—I would leap, sky-dive if I could!
And now the winds whirl screaming
So near to New Year's Eve
We would run away, but daren't leave
For this place is where we need be
If any dead sons, parachutes reversed
Are to raise their voices
From stark caskets, urns and dust
From the iron star's unsleeping rust,
To sing to you to me,
If any dead hearts
Should beat or burn
If there be any new truth
We might yet learn--
Curious as any mountain cat--
If any horseman head in hand,
Hand on hat,
Does not pass by, after all, but pauses:
To listen, to speak, to draw near.
To see what new revealing blaze
May vault that silent, smoking wall of fear.

DOROTHY (DOTTIE) PAYNE

I WILL NOT WRITE A POEM TODAY

I will not write a poem today:
I will not wring my hands in grief,
pound my fist on the wall
or call on you to pray.
     I will not write a poem today.

I will not post my outrage
on my Facebook page,
or call a congressperson
to complain.

I will not write an editorial
full of facts about the history
     of lynching:
I will not even mention
Emmet, Oscar, Sandra, or Breonna's names.

Nor will I rage at home alone;
    I will remember them,
    kneel beside Kap and honor them.
    I will say their names out loud in every
         crowd;
    I will Holler "Earl Grant!", "Earl Grant!"
    at every liberal politician's chant:
"Wait, we can fix this!"

Nor will I ask God to
forgive or stop this
for this is not his fault;
    only Evil does this,
    only Evil.

No,
I will not write a poem, or
go on a fast;
I will no longer answer the call
from those who have no action plan
to stop this.

Nor will I let my children,
my friends,
my neighbors,
my co-workers,
the grieving mothers,
the homeless and alone,
the sick and lonely,
desperate refugees,
caged babies,
incarcerated innocents,
the underfed,
unclothed,
hungry,
destitute
unhoused
and unemployed
              ever forget this.

I will not turn the other cheek,
will not fail to speak out,
or call this anything but what it is:
      A crime
      A crime against another black man/woman
      A crime against everyone who looks like the guilty.
      A crime against the children, and the children's
                                      children:
      A crime against humanity!

I will not grovel with reason before the indifferent;
I will no longer believe that those who remain silent
are not complicit;
I refuse to make peace with this.

But I will come with you,
to start anew;
I will stand alongside you,
make an army of minions
--the deserving-ones--
just as those before us have done:
>   I will be an ally:
>   forthright and fierce,
>   solid and strong!

But I will not write a poem about this.

POET E SPOKEN

WAITING TO EXHALE

They dropped tear gas and
Hung a few ropes in garages
And I can't count the number that swung on trees
Collected six souls last week in a Nation
That has wrapped its fabric of hate
Around my innocents
Swore allegiance to a badge
So now laws are paper thin
But where seeds fall
Roots of change are planted in
And those I can't breathe signs
In those Oakland Hills are priceless
As another baby is murdered at a protest
Civil unrest and you can attest
That the only time I see you giving air hugs
Is when something happens
So I hope this clears your conscience you see
I saw signs that said say their names
But we all know in a few short years that
They shall become nameless
But I saw traces of Yuseph and Trayvon
When Ahmaud was running and
The words of Rodney
Must have rung out for Mario
Because although in a chair and handcuffed
They still kept punching his identity
And you don't need trees
To hang in a jail cell
So I cried out for my sister Sandra
And wondered did it take 41 shots to kill Breonna
And why was Tamir shot for playing with a toy gun

When Nikolas had a real one
He shot up 17 but left the scene breathing
While Wille and Rayshard were both killed in drive-thrus
Like drive bys
So fuck your all lives matter signs!
So after my sip
I poured some out for the 400 years
Stuffed the rag in my cocktail
And burned your shit
Because we are tired of being your "Targets"
But it didn't take 45 but a minute
To call the National Guards in
Might even drop bombs on unarmed civilians
Justify the homicides by insurrections
Another SunDown Town you can't even walk in
From Tulsa, Georgia, Minnesota,
Wilmington, Staten Island, and Oakland
Yes this whole entire Nation
I swear Grandpa Halsey sometimes
I feel like the candle is burning from both ends
But as a child of Obatala
Given the breath of life
By Olodumare I spit fire
In the name of truth and justice
For all those you thought you silenced
When I EXHALE!!!!

GREGORY POND

THIS PATH WE'RE ON

our planet is crumbling under us
we think we stand on terra firma
but instead it's liquid, sand and dust
so the next steps we take are never sure
never certain or feel secure enough
we're humans linked
to water and land
who don't realize
that divided we sink
but united we can
though this path we're on
of self-destruct
leaves us ripe for annihilation
though less by space invasion
than by our own hands

existence was supposed to be easy
loving in good and plenty
but with all we've been given
too many still living on empty
too many too driven by greed
who find it easy keeping score
in a world that profits and feeds
on the bones of those most in need
through famine, oppression and war

we trick, we track, we frick, we frack,
kill life where we find it
and we don't look back
even while sliding off melting ice
and stumbling off eroding shores

this path we're on
of infected skies and deeper freeze
poisoned oceans and global warm
will leave a world of such extremes
burned by sun or drowned in rising seas
where humans beings and other species
will cease to swim, fly, crawl, walk or breathe
any longer

KATHY POWERS

**WE OPPRESSED DREAMERS
LIVE IN THE RIGHT TIME.**

Bring in the love lights.
Bring justice.
Bring hope.

Use courage.
Use our inside and outside voices.
Use one's rights.

As we are all life stakeholders.
We are stronger together.

THORWALD PROLL *(Germany)*

DAS ENDE DES ZWANZIGSTEN JAHRHUNDERTS

*Die Bäume zersplitterten
wie einfache* Streichhölzer

*Pferde hatten sich in die Fahrstühle
geflüchtet*

Bis zum Duft des Abends
schloss ich die Augen danach
warf ich den Schlüssel fort

Der Mond glaubt wirklich
er ist nichts als ein normaler
Stern den man einfach auch so
anbellen kann

*Eine Kleinigkeit ganz stofflicher
Art* fiel mir auf
die Verkäuferin war vollkommen
nackt

Ich trage einen Brief an Dich
schon lange mit mir herum
und was mich traurig stimmt
jetzt auf dem Weg

zum Briefkasten sind allein Wahlunterlagen
das Streusalz unter meinen Füßen

> *einige der Zeilen, markiert als Kursizeilen,
> wurden von Louis Aragon (1897-1982) geschrieben,
> und inspirierten mich zu dem ganzen Gedicht.
> Die Übersetzung ins Deutsche stammt von
> Heribert Becker.

THORWALD PROLL *(Germany)*

THE END OF THE TWENTIETH CENTURY

The trees splintered
like simple matches

Horses had fled themselves
into the elevators

Until the scent of the evening
I closed my eyes
afterwards I threw away
the key

The moon really believes
he is nothing but a normal star
you just like that
can bark at, too

A little something more
material kind of
caught my eye
the saleswoman was completely
naked

I carry a letter to you
been with me for a long time
and what saddens me
now on the way

to the mailbox
are only voting documents
the road salt under my feet

> *some of the lines marked as italic lines,
> were written by Louis Aragon (1897-1982),
> and inspired me to write the whole poem.
> The German translation is from Heribert Becker.
> *(Translated from German by the author)*

SANDRO SARDELLA *(Italy)*

BLUE NIGHT POSTCARDS DISCANTO

"Stai attento alle tue orecchie, esse hanno dei muri."
        (scritta su un muro di Parigi nel 1968)

1
il prezzo degli aquiloni salirà alle stelle
vibrano i cadaveri dissanguati di vuote automobili
traboccano di fiamma   l'odore di piscio
respirare la brezza dei relitti   le raffiche di piombo
dei venti di Libia   le canzoni le parlate
roventi novelle spedite da tradite primavere
uno stagno di chiacchere   la parola affonda
nella pagina la farfalla cascata nel bicchiere
mare petrolio guasto   s'è imbriacata
la polvere dei davanzali di Taranto arrugginisce il fiato
di bimbi nel cortile della scuola
l'alveare vuoto senza api senza miele   abbandonato

2
Racconto   Raccontami
dell'ascoltare i colori delle foglie
della città dei cementi dentro un'epoca di mercenari
del barcollare alla cieca nella notte italiana
dei fiori che si allungano verso la luce
del sapore della nebbia

3
il silenzio ha un suono agro
le foto carbone e luce di Salgado
splendono d'amaro
medicano la tristessa della foresta
le stelle bucano il buio predatorio del giardino umano
nel cielo una risata è comparsa e se n'è andata

SANDRO SARDELLA *(Italy)*

BLUE NIGHT POSTCARDS DESCANT

"Watch out for your ears. They have walls."
        —Street graffiti, Paris 1968

1
the price of kites will skyrocket
hum the drained corpses of empty automobiles
boiling over with flames   stench of piss
inhaling the breeze of wreckage   barrage of lead
Libyan winds   the songs the talks
incandescent novellas out of betrayed springtimes
stagnant chit-chat   words sink
into the page a butterfly has fallen into the drink
broken down petrol sea   she got drunk
the dust of Taranto's windowsills rusts the breath
of children in the school courtyard
empty beehive with no bees or honey   abandoned

2
I tell   Do tell
of listening to the color of leaves
of the city of concrete in a time of mercenaries
of staggering blind through the Italian night
of flowers stretching toward the light
of the flavor of fog

3
silence tastes sour
Salgado's light and carbon prints
shimmer with bitterness
medicating the sorrow of the forest
stars puncture the predatory darkness in this human garden
up in the sky a laugh appeared then was gone

l'ombra della grafite cenere s'insinua investe
plasma l'invadenza virale prepotente di
nascosti chiarori di   nascoste verità
smorfie e sorrisi e croci sulla sabbia di Rio

4
cosa fanno i garofani rossi che non si stancano di
ondeggiare che continuano ad accompagnare
l'utopia che non finisce mai cosa fanno i garofani
rossi che   domani mi innamoro

5
tenevo un fiore rosso nella mano nera di
un catarroso blues tra le ali unte e rumorose del
lavoro salariato   la fabbrica bolliva ansimava
le mie mani   profumava di sesso
una vecchia bandiera tra ferrivecchi e catrame
ho visto la santa rigida tuta operaia lacerarsi
ho visto inchiostri ritornare in aule saccenti
volevo concimare con la poesia il lavoro
volevo rompere il potere della sirena del padrone

6
la pelle della luce la vastità dell'ombra di una foglia
Vergogna a coloro che sputano sulla generazione di
Greta Thumberg e di Vanessa Nakate
Vergogna Vergogna ai messaggeri ai santificatori
dell'economico
Aprire le porte con Don Cherry che soffia
la voce umana nella tromba
Aprire il respiro lungo i fraseggi del sax di Lester Young
Aprire le note blues piano di Thelonious Monk in
"Round about midnight"
Aprire all' "Andare Camminare Lavorare e Altri Discorsi"
nel bicchiere vuotato di Piero Ciampi

the shadow of graphite ashes creeps overtakes
molds the overbearing viral intrusiveness of
hidden gleamings of   hidden truths
grimaces and smiles and crosses across the sand in Rio

4
what do the red carnations do as they never tire of
swaying continuing to accompany
the never-ending utopia what do the red
carnations do   tomorrow I'm falling in love

5
I kept a red flower in the black hand of
a mucous blues between the oily noisy wings of
wage labor   the factory boiled panted
my hands   it was fragrant with sex
an old flag between scrap metal and tar
I saw the holy rigid factory overalls be lacerated
I saw ink return to know-it-all chambers
I wanted to fertilize work with poetry
I wanted to shatter the power of the masters' siren

6
the skin the light the vastness of the shadow of one leaf
Shame on those who spit on the generation of
Greta Thunberg and Vanessa Nakate
Shame Shame upon the messengers the sanctifiers
of economics
Opening doors with Don Cherry blowing
a human voice into the trumpet
Opening breath along the sax phrasings of Lester Young
Opening blue piano notes of Thelonious Monk in
"Round about midnight"
Opening "Going Walking Working and Other Speeches"
in the emptied glass of Piero Ciampi

Aprire il mare delle tue labbra
    la mia febbre   la mia linea d'indifferenza
Aprire a tutto fiato   a tutto corpo
la pelle della luce la castità dell'ombra di una foglia
sulla sabbia nera   giù fra le nuvole
fiori spenti   dentro un cielo di Lombardia

7
Racconto   Raccontami
delle magre parole rubate depurate dalla discarica mediatica
del vento rivoltoso nel rantolante rabbioso deserto urbano
della giovane poeta che scrive nelle cicatrici della filosofia
dello note spettinate e parlanti dei vinti oltre un presente di
devastamento di paura di guerre di di di di di di di

Opening the sea of your lips
       my fever   my line of indifference
Opening with full breath   full body
the skin the light the chasteness of the shadow of one leaf
on the black sand   down through the clouds
spent flowers under a Lombardy sky

7
I tell   Do tell
of meager stolen words purified out of the media
of the wind rioting through the rabid rattling urban desert
of the young poet writing into the scars of philosophy
of the disheveled chatty notes of the vanquished beyond a present of
devastation of fear of war of of of of of of of

(Translated from Italian by Lapo Guzzini)

LUÍS FILIPE SARMENTO *(Portugal)*

REFUGIA-TE

Refugia-te na tua consciência, sem cruzes nem crescentes,
sem arames nem muros, sem farpas nem ódios; e logo
                                        reconhecerás
entre as multidões de andarilhos que perpassam a tua
                                        memória
os teus ascendentes vindos de longe que te fizeram nascer
                                        aqui.
De onde vens? A que caverna original pertences? Que
                                        línguas
navegam nos mares e nos rios do teu sangue? Quantos
                                        deuses
adoraste, pedindo e esperando que o futuro não fosse
                                        este presente?
Onde estão as divinas respostas?
Refugia-te na tua consciência, sem o medo que os
                                        sacerdotes
do poder oculto te querem impor nem a angústia do
                                        sonho destruído.
Observa a renovação do mar, a regeneração do planeta
a cada ataque inconsciente dos loucos e logo verás
o poder das entranhas deste grandioso globo
como se fosse uma cabeça que pensa que a possibilidade
da derrota é a impossibilidade da vida e faz renascer
em todo o esplendor o mapa colorido do que na realidade
                                        somos:
refugia-te na tua consciência como anfitrião do futuro
e não temas os deuses, eles que são divinos que se
                                        entendam
longe desta terra, e abre as portas do teu humilde casebre
como se fosse um palácio contra a morte
e contra a babélica imagem do fim.

LUÍS FILIPE SARMENTO *(Portugal)*

TAKE REFUGE

Take refuge in your conscience, without crosses or crescents,
without wires or walls, without barbs or hatreds; and you will
                                                soon recognize
among the crowds of wanderers that permeate your memory
your ancestors from afar who gave birth to you here.
Where do you come from? To which original cave do you
                                        belong? What languages
sail the seas and rivers of your blood? How many gods
did you worship, asking and hoping that the future would not be
                                                  this present?
Where are the divine answers?
Take refuge in your conscience, without the fear that priests
of hidden power want to impose on you nor the anguish of the
                                                  destroyed dream.
Observe the renewal of the sea, the regeneration of the planet,
every unconscious attack of the madman, and you will soon see
the power of the bowels of this magnificent globe,
as if it were a head that thinks the possibility
of defeat is the impossibility of life and makes it reborn
in all its splendor, the colorful map of what we really are:
take refuge in your conscience as host of the future
and do not fear the gods, who are divine and who understand
                                                  each other
far from this Earth, and open the doors of your humble hovel
as if it were a palace against death
and against the chaotic image of the end.

        (Translated from Portuguese by Scott Edward Anderson)

NINA SERRANO

LAST DAYS OF FEBRUARY 2022

We were at the end of our walk
along the shore of Green Island
approaching our car in the parking lot
Three rabbits raced across the field
hopping like early metaphors of spring
Further away were a group of walkers like us
with picker uppers and trash bags removing the trash
They too seemed like metaphors
This was first time we saw others cleaning up here
I felt the hope of the upcoming spring
With our picker uppers and trash bags
are we too multiplying like rabbits?

KIM SHUCK

CLIMATE CHANGE

Perfect moment
Between night and morning
Tree gossip
In chemical syllables
On the porch
I listen with my
Jackhammer hearing my
Numb nose
Like music through a wall
Arc of a year
Measured in order
Rise and fall of temperature
Flavor of light from day to day
There are beings who know that things have changed
Press
Into the hillside
For the memory of creek
Memory of fire skitters along
Bark and branch tip
Beings who know that things are changing
Slow inhale
Slow exhale
Beings committed to location
To community
Who sing in these hours
Sing the confusion
Of broken expectations

DINOS SIOTIS / ΝΤΙΝΟ ΣΙΩΤΗΣ *(Greece)*

Ο ΚΟΣΜΟΣ ΤΟ 2022

Ένας κόσμος τρελός, τυφλωμένος από αδυναμία,
ζει όλη του τη ζωή σαν να πεθαίνει, υπάρχει αρκετή
δημόσια κατάντια, κατήφορος και σκάνδαλα, οι ελίτ
οι πολιτικές δεν θέλουν ούτε να δουν ή ν' ακούσουν
ούτε να αισθανθούν τον παλμό των απελπισμένων

ανθρώπων, μόνο θέλουν να κυριαρχήσουν και να
συσσωρεύουν χρήμα και πλούτο για την άρχουσα
τάξη, έτσι ο λαός έχει θρησκεία χωρίς θεό, βιβλία
χωρίς σελίδες, παιδεία χωρίς σχολεία, νοσοκομεία
χωρίς νοσηλευτές, γιατρούς, θεραπεία, πορτοφόλια

χωρίς χρήματα, εργασία χωρίς ασφάλιση υγείας,
υπάρχουν πολλές ψυχικές ασθένειες στη δημόσια
ζωή και μπόλικο τσιμέντο, αρκετά για έναν πύργο
νέο της Βαβέλ που δεν θα ανέβει αλλά εκεί κάτω,
στα έγκατα της γης, να συναντήσει τους άστεγους,

καταραμένους, τους πεινασμένους, τους άνεργους,
να τους ξυπνήσει, να τους αναστήσει, να τους κάνει
πηδήξουν από τους τάφους για να πάρουν τα όπλα,
να νικήσουν τις βδέλλες της δημόσιας σφαίρας, να
δώσει δύναμη κι ελπίδα στον εξαντλημένο πλανήτη

DINOS SIOTIS *(Greece)*

THE WORLD IN 2022

A desperate world blinded by helplessness, it lives
out its whole life as if it is dying, there is abundant
public downstream, downhill and downbeat, the
political elites neither want to see nor hear nor to
feel the pulse of the desperate people, only want

to dominate and accumulate money and wealth
for the ruling class, so the people have religion
without god, books without pages, schools without
education, hospitals without nurses, doctors or a
treatment, wallets without money, work without

health insurance, there is plenty of mental illness
in the public life and plenty of cement, enough
for a new tower of Babel that will not go up but
down there, in the bowels of the earth, to meet
the damned, the homeless, the hungry, the poor,

the unemployed, the unprivileged, to awaken
them, to resurrect them and to rise up, to make
them jump from their graves, to take up arms, to
defeat the leeches of the public sphere, to give
power and hope to the exhausted planet Earth

(Translated from Greek by the author)

DOREEN STOCK

WHO WILL TALLY

Who will tally
in this first sunrise
of the new year

as it moves across the USA

the hospitals of covid patients, the gunned down
being laid to earth, the charred remains of newly-
torched houses covered by a sudden snow and the
paths of the two tornados, the underpasses shielding
tent encampments from the rain, the empty bellies
shivering, the overdosed, and those who believe
that the President was never elected?

and who will tally

the quiet joys eating breakfast
smiles breaking out at the sight
of a landscape spared, a loved face,
the students of change in their serious glasses
the birds splashing in rain-filled bathes?

Who will report the tally?
What will they say
as Desmond Tutu and Betty White
are laid to rest, only two of many,

who will tally
the rest, who will report, and what will be
said to build, to destroy? And like the many-
armed goddess who holds the souls

of the dead on one side of her slender, belled
body, the souls of the living on the other

how will we turn with her this day
to build as the clouds do
the sound of bells, tinkling,
and to destroy, the sound of bells, tolling,
weeping at what holy fires
have turned to ash?

SARAH THILYKOU *(Greece)*

ΦΩΤΙΕΣ

Είμαι το αρχέγονο δάσος
ο αναστεναγμός του ανέμου μες στα φύλλα
ρομφαία αχτίδα
η αρκούδα με βήμα βαρύ
ξερά κλαδιά που ηχούν στο πέρασμά της
είμαι
η μοναξιά του λύκου
το βλέμμα του ελαφιού
το ράμφισμα του δρυοκολάπτη

η θρυαλλίδα που βάζει φωτιά

SARAH THILYKOU *(Greece)*

FIRES

I am the primitive forest
the sigh of the wind in the leaves
a sword of rays
a bear with a heavy footstep
dry branches crackling when it passes
I am
the loneliness of the wolf
the glance of the deer
the pecking of the woodpecker

I am
also the fuse -
setting the forest on fire

(Translated from Greek by the author)

Sandro Sardella

MATTHEW TALEBI

MOTHER EARTH TALKS

The ancient glistening Glaciers,
in the north and the south, woke up astonished
 Weeping.
Long-lived velvet snow on the Himalayas,
 Melting.
The little rainbow glass fish,
 Fearing the unknown.
and the playful giant whales jumping up and down,
 Complaining.
Buzzing bees and singing birds flying over prairies,
Searching to find shadows of the sun.
Speechless horses and cattle,
 unable to raise their voices in tears,
 Contesting.
All oceans waters detesting,
deadly alien plastics.
Flowers on serene plateaus of Asia,
Having lost their erotic aroma.
 Now questing.
The entire existence of the only,
 blue planet of love and beauty,
 in the milky way.
*Crying out,
 Pleading,*

*With the two-legged ambitious creature.
The pretender, the destroyer.*

RAYMOND NAT TURNER

RECLAIMING OUR TIME
FOR THE PLANET...

Grand Canyon bathtub rings telling
us the Colorado River's dropped over
150 feet. Twenty years of drought—And
A wildfire a week; A nor'easter; super-
storm; hurricane; tornado; typhoon; And
tsunami over blackened birds, slimy, gooey,
tar balled waters—obligatory oil spills over
Corporate propaganda cycles—A delicious
recipe for disaster...

Whisker-sized particulate matter's winning
Air superiority in pumpkin skies. Same skies
Bees buzzed decks from; Skies hummingbirds
and butterflies hung out in.
Skies crows dropped from, jamming with
pigeons and spying on stashing/noshing
squirrels. A place where you could get a
gallon of unleaded water that smelled drinkable...

This was before Roundup Ready corporate
propaganda cycles ejaculating Satan's sperm
into our aquifers. Before prioritizing our
Friends by stages/types of cancer they suffer...

No need for nuance here—let's say it simply—
say it plainly:
the kettle's been on the back burner whistling
Frantically for decades—Warning of capitalist
immolation...And the world can't wait!!

The world can't wait...Bassackwards...
for 21st century technology to catch
up with 17th century ideology—can't

wait in perpetuity on old
mush-mouthed men's mumblings on markets—
Seventeenth century
catechisms covering 21st century climate crimes...

The world can't wait...
for more inflated claptrap; more cleverly crafted
lies—more methane promises huffed and puffed—
Killing us softly with their carbon...

The world can't wait...
on fossil fools/clean coal clowns dancing spastic 2/4 Dances that
donkey-elephants dance across aisles—externalizing excrement;
Leaving dung-splattered streets like irresponsible circuses...

The world can't wait...
on predators bearing bars, concertina wire, cardboard
mattresses and tents within shadows of scaffolding and
                                         cranes—
Can't wait on Lilliputian politicians/jingoist gangsters/greasy-
thumbed grifters doubling as junk metal-chested generals
disguised as the golden calf-tethered to tits on the Wall Street
bull blocking and stalling! Waging war by another name...

No summer space get away—Earth's home—we need its crystal
clear, pure water, cedar fresh air;
Not rectangular rags/jagged lines/bottom lines on bloodstained
paper

We need street heat—shoe leather legislators. We need
                                         pavement
policymakers who, at least, will stop sullying our good names
                                         with
climate criminal's crimes.
We must at least learn to Say Their Names—connecting
Wall Street gangs to climate crimes: Superstorm Chevron;
Nor' easter Exxon; Tsunami Shell; blackened bird BP; et. al.

DAVID VOLPENDESTA

FORBIDDEN PSALM TO CLIMATE CHANGE

It's more insidious
than climate change,
It's a pen dripping spilled ink
on a white silk blouse.
It's gasoline spilled on a wedding cake.

Football is an enemy of life.
It's the best friend of capitalism
particularly Super Bowl Sunday,
which is also the day many women are beaten
by their husbands or boyfriends
or Joe Six-pack.
People say they're having a good time,
but greedy football owners make the money
while so many others die

Yeah, Super Bowl Sunday
when everyone goes to church
and then files into I-Hop for pancakes,
sausages, whipped cream, coffee,
and three big slices of lemon pie.

Three blocks down from I-Hop
is a liquor store where everyone picks up
a twelve-pack of Budweiser
and a quart of Old Grand-Dad.

At lunch it's two hours to game time and
VIP husbands and boyfriends
start to slap their women around.

Now the big game will start in an hour,
featuring two star running backs:
the murderous Vladimir Putin
and his fat buddy, Donald Trump,
both coached by the Hall of Shame quarterback,
the master of climate change, the devil!

OSCAR SAAVEDRA VILLARROEL *(Chile)*

CHILEAN CAPITALISM AND FAMILY

Imagine an empty house. Imagine that in its empty interior there are many cages. Imagine that each cage is in the roar of a tiger. Imagine that tiger dancing on TV. Imagine that the TV is therefore a cage. Imagine the cage turning into your tongue. Imagine your language inside the cage. Imagine the tiger-your language-the cage. Imagine that a family buys the emptiness of such house. Imagine that the family is made of a father, a mother, two children, and a grandmother. Imagine that the grandmother gets a plastic surgery on her tongue. Imagine her plastic language. Imagine the mother to follow the steps of the grandmother. Imagine the father going into debt to cost this path. Imagine the tiger to devour the father's wallet. Imagine the father stepping into a reality show. Now imagine the tiger and the father eating lunch on television. Imagine the children day and night watching the show on television. Imagine that the cages are the seats for the father and the tiger. Imagine a family devoured by the tiger.. Imagine the tiger inside a children's tale.

CATHLEEN WILLIAMS

ON THE HILL
    After Nazim Hikmet

broken, abandoned lands, torn edges of cities
    where people live outside
air belongs to all of this, air into the lungs of all
    even the ravens, the somber crows

air washed by the grasses that force their way
    into the humblest crevice
sparrows' high-pitched voices breaking out
    carried away by the air

it all counts, even the fly tiptoeing, tiptoeing
    by my elbow, down a blade
a cluster of clovers, almost too tiny to exist
    a cloud, an invisible weave

oh, as a child, friendly with weeds, the roar
    of dandelions
abalone shells, the inside, then rain
    on spring horizon

the spiral of moth, the silk of web –
    each touch of air
tests and shines, falcon wings like knives
    all this, plays, turns, tries

true, my love, the body long ago was claimed
    as their machine
yes, I can feel the seams where my heart
    has been broken

I listen to Nakim, here now, here forever,
        this is our time of need
come now, heal us with your breath, speak –
        poet, speak to us

"Believe in seeds, earth, and the sea
        But people above all
Love clouds, machines, and books
        But people above all ..."

D.A. "ROARSHOCK" WILSON

AN EXCERPT FROM "THE ASBESTOS FILES"

The asbestos files:
each one contains
a working man's tragedy.
They did their jobs
each day for decades
cutting sheet metal
fitting pipes
installing insulation welding together
the nation's infrastructure
while unknowingly breathing asbestos fibers
which worked at their lungs
year after year
until cancers grew
and devoured them.
A galaxy of names
dates of birth and marriage
ominous dates of diagnosis
asbestosis fibrosis
pulmonary disease
lung cancer, other cancers
often dates of death while waiting
for the insurance settlement to clear.
And no one gets paid
without a proper social security
number.
Disputed asbestosis.
The legal fees will always be paid.
And a lesser settlement
given to those who smoked
because lung disease
can also be caused by cigarettes.

Tobacco
another great
American commodity
black smoke.
Some say asbestos
others say asbestus
Some say
the unquenchable stone,
inextinguishable
fabled dragon's fires.
asbestic armor
made from
an alleged kind
of incombustible
flax,
nor does it conduct
electricity.
Asbestos is a mineral,
a natural substance,
unlike petrochemical plastics,
a silicate of
calcium and magnesium
which occurs in long
greyish thread-like fibers.
The finest asbestos
distinguished by
long silky pearly white fibers
when broken up
it makes a dust
of tiny fibers
when ingested
they remain in the body
thereafter.
Asbestiform:
the form of this poem.

Asbestos was found
in the body
of Esther's first husband
after his untimely
unexplained death
"From when he was
in the Navy."
A matrix
operation
quality of life
interferes with MY
quality of life.
Food Not Bombs!
When I unloaded trucks
of insulated heater pipes
once a week for several years
died yellow dust
tickling through
a surgical mask.
So am I
a walking
time bomb?
Working files lung pain
the power of suggestion
I am, perhaps, Asbestine:
not likely to take fire.

XIAO-XIAO 潇潇 *(China)*

七月飞雪

  潇潇

7月27日12点12分
点开抖音，一个寒冷的声音
把我冻着了

抖音号61355452的男人
打着寒颤，哆嗦着叨叨：
"2020年7月26号
北京下雪啦
太冷了，冻死我了！"

雾蒙蒙的镜头
公路两旁茂密的树叶上
挂满了雪花
摇晃着，哈着粗气

我坐在昨日还是35度的家里
一阵鸡皮疙瘩骤起
喷嚏不断，清鼻涕长流
面巾纸像大雪片扔了一地

我搜索这一天的黄历
宜：寒穴、结网、安葬
忌：诸事不宜。如今
是气候疯了？还是城市已

XIAO XIAO 潇潇 *(China)*

JULY SNOW 七月的飞雪

On July 27, at 12:12,
I open Tiktok
and a cold voice
freezes me

The guy who's Tiktok #61355452
is trembling and chattering:
"On July 26, 2020,
It snowed in Beijing
It's too cold, I'm freezing!"

In the foggy lens
the dense leaves on both sides of the highway
are covered in snow
swaying, breathing heavily

I'm sitting in my house where it's still 95 degrees
A wave of goose bumps suddenly rises
I sneeze constantly, clearing the flowing mucous
Tissues are thrown all over the floor like giant snowflakes

I search today's almanac
Appropriate: fix the hole, weave a fishing net, bury the
                                                                                       dead
Taboo: Everything is inappropriate
Is it that the climate has gone mad? Or that the city
                                                                                        already is

(Translated from Chinese by Jami Proctor Xu)

ANDRENA ZAWINSKI

NIGHT MUSIC, A WHALE SONG

Against the sail masts' offbeat taps onto each other,
bay bells mixing in with tinny harbor chimes,
distant buoys throwing their soft moans to the wind,

all of them singing to the moon in a whale-like croon
that bellows love songs from the seabed floor,

I am swept back to my first whale sighting,
the young humpback's notes rippling out
before it hit the headland, its shroud of sound lost to sea.

Rocked by waves, stranded beneath the blue moon
at Point Bonita, everything turned a deadly quiet

where high winds once rammed ships cliffside
dumping potatoes, lumber, cotton, gold, all of it
sunk into the deep, unlike the ballooning beached corpse

in descending light, tonight its heft of ghost at my side,
pressing hard into me the tremendous weight of sea.

BIOGRAPHICAL NOTES

INDRAN AMIRTHANAYAGAM's new book is *Ten Thousand Steps Against The Tyrant* (BroadstoneBooks, 2022). He has published twenty-two books and writes in English, French, Spanish, Haitian Creole and Portuguese. He publishes poetry at Beltway Editions (www.beltwayeditions.com) and at The Beltway Poetry Quarterly (www.beltwaypoetry.com).

AYO AYOOLA-AMALE is a poet, artist, author, and director of Splendors of Dawn Poetry Foundation. She is acknowledged as a poet for positive social change. Her poems are concerned with confronting the problem of violence, racism, and the breakdown of human community.

LISBIT BAILEY, a San Francisco poet, is a member of the Revolutionary Poets Brigade and has been one of the editors for the 2021 and 2022 editions of this anthology.

MAHNAZ BADIHIAN Is a poet and artist. She has an MFA from Pacific U, an MA from Baltimore U, and a DDS from the University of Iowa. Badihian published many books of poetry in Farsi, English, and translations. She edited Plague2020, poetry and art from around the world. Her latest collection of poems, *Ask The Wind,* was published in 2022. She runs Mahmag.org

KEMLYN TAN BAPPE is a multi-disciplinary artist from Singapore, and a special education teacher in Arizona. She is the director of Q's BLUE WORLD, host of "Between The Lines," and recipient of the VSA Teaching Artist Fellowship 2009, and presented at the Smithsonian Museum of American Art.

VIRGINIA BARRETT is a poet, writer, artist, editor, and educator. Her six books of poetry include *Between Looking* (Finishing Line Press, 2019) and *Crossing Haight*—San Francisco poems (Jambu Press, 2018).

JUDITH AYN BERNHARD Is the author of the poetry collection, *Prisoners of Culture* and a book of short stories, *Marriages.* A former Berlitz School of Languages instructor and translator, her literary translations and poems have appeared in numerous anthologies. She lives with her husband, Byron Spooner, in San Francisco where she teaches writing and occasionally gives public readings of her work.

SCOTT BIRD is a poet, painter and musician in San Francisco and a member of the Revolutionary Poets Brigade. His artistic work focuses on the queer experience and working-class struggle. He's organized the covers and visual artwork for this issue, with Agneta Falk. He is also the creator of the Maybird Project www.themaybirdproject.com.

CHARLES CURTIS BLACKWELL is a writer currently working on a forthcoming book titled *The Eye in Us*. His visual arts have been shown from coast to coast. Charles teaches creative writing at Youth Spirit Art Works.

DAN BRADY Is a poet, teacher, and a writer of science fiction and children's books. He's long been active in the San Francisco poetry scene: performing at and hosting readings, publishing, and keeping a calendar of open mic poetry readings.

DANIEL BROOKS Is a writer, poet, and editor. He received an MA in sociology from Arizona State University and is a special education teacher in his hometown. His work has appeared in the Indianapolis Review, Hawai'i Review, People's Tribune, Kallatumba Press, and more.

KRISTINA BROWN is a writer, painter, and poet. She often writes about what people will, and will not, do for love. She is a co-editor of this anthology.

JEREMY CANTOR's debut collection is *Wisteria From Seed* (Kelsay Books). He began writing after retiring from a career in laboratory chemistry. He has made and tested engine oil additives, detergents, and pharmaceuticals, driven a forklift, worked in a full-body acid-proof hazmat suit, tried to keep his fingers working in a walk-in freezer at -40°F, and worked behind radiation shielding. He prefers writing.

YOLANDA CATZALCO is a Mexican American poet who lives in San Francisco. She advocates for the homeless, the undocumented immigrants, especially essential workers, and for addressing climate warming.

MARCO CINQUE writes, photographs, plays ethnic instruments, recites, publishes essays, poetry collections, articles. He has published more than 30 books and has been translated into English, Spanish, Albanian, and French.

BOBBY COLEMAN is Managing Editor of Jambu Press, San Francisco, co-founder of the Revolutionary Poets Brigade, and a co-editor of this anthology.

FRANCIS COMBES is one of the most politically engaged poets in Paris and all of France. He is coordinator of the WPM for Europe and the leader of a group of French poets, Le Merle moqueur, which is the French group of the WPM.

KITTY COSTELLO's collection *Upon Waking: New & Selected Poems 1977-2017* gathers 40 years of her San Francisco writings. She is co-editor of the new anthology *Muslim American Writers at Home: Stories, Essays & Poems of Identity, Diversity & Belonging*, helping to overturn Islamophobia.

J. VERN CROMARTIE's poetry has appeared in The Black Panther; The Journal of Pan African Studies; Unity; Current; C; Haight-Ashbury Literary Journal; The Black Times; Grassroots; WarpLand; and Afrikan Perspectives, and in the anthologies: *Ascension I; Ascension II; The Otherwise Room; Street Meeting; Would You Wear My Eyes? A Tribute to Bob Kaufman;* and *Overthrowing Capitalism*. His latest book is *Intercommunal Street Poems*.

ANITA ODENA CRUZ is a member of Hayward's B Street Writers Collective and Bay Area Poets Coalition, won first place prizes for Make a Living as a Poet and Edith, and read at Jack Hirschman's Poets 11 for Bayview, SF.

ROMEO ALCALA CRUZ writes poetry in both English and Bicol (rawit dawit.) He has written two books, *Washing Rice and* *other Poems* and *Crossing the River from Memory to Forgetfulness*. He recites at Dan Brady's reading at Sacred Grounds Cafe and likes "The Emperor of Ice Cream."

JOHN CURL's latest book is *Rainbow Weather: Poems for Environmental Healing*, scheduled to be out in the fall of 2022 from Vagabond Books. He recorded his poetry this year for the spoken poetry web site Voetica.com. He is a co-editor of this anthology. www.johncurl.net

AMIT DAHIYABADSHAH has made his living from poetry for the past 25 years. His 21st collection,*The Tiger Poet New and Selected Poems* has just been published in the U.S. He believes poetry will help "Change" not through great poets and great poetry, but more poets and more poetry, ie: the poetry of "We the People."

CAROL DENNEY is a Berkeley cartoonist, poet, and musician who wrote "Internet Sensation" after getting an emailed poem from fellow poet and comrade Gary Hicks.

GERMAIN DROOGENBROODT is a Belgian poet living in Spain, translator and promoter of international poetry. He was nominated in 2017 for the Nobel Prize in Literature. According to Chinese critics, his poetry is TAO and ZEN

CARLOS RAUL DUFFLAR is a poet, playwright, activist, and member of the New York Revolutionary Poets Brigade, and celebrating 27 years of The Bread is Rising Poetry Collective.

MARIA J. ESTRADA is a professor of composition, literature, and creative writing. She grew up in the desert outside of Yuma, Arizona, in the real Barrio de los Locos. She writes like a loca every minute she can, while magically balancing her work and her wonderfully supportive husband, remarkable children, and menagerie of animals. She lives in Chicago.

AGNETA FALK Is a member of the World Poetry Movement and the San Francisco RPB and is preparing her third major volume of poetry for publication. She organized the covers and art works for this issue, with Scott Bird.

MAURO FFORTISSIMO is an Argentinian/Italian/American musician, painter, poet, and activist living in the Bay Area. Born in 1962, he moved to the US in 1980.

MARK FISHBEIN graduated from CCNY in 1971, followed by a maîtrise from the Sorbonne in literature. His latest collection of poetry is *Reflections in the Time of Trumpius Maximus*, (Atmosphere Press, 2021). He hosts Planet Poetry 28. Known as "poet with guitar," Mark also plays professionally.

MARCOS DE SOUSA FREITAS Is a poet, engineer, and environmental and cultural activist. He lives in Brasilia and is the author of *In The Coming Afternoon*. He is a member of the National Association of Writers (ANE) and Brazilian Union of Writers (UBE).

RAFAEL JESUS GONZALEZ, four times nominated for a Pushcart Prize, was honored in 2015 by the city of Berkeley with a Lifetime Achievement Award. In 2017 he was named the first Poet Laureate of Berkeley. He is a former Earth First! journal poetry editor and 20-year Green Party county commissioner.

ART GOODTIMES, poet, basket weaver, and former Green party elected official in Colorado, served as San Miguel County commissioner (1996-2016) and Western Slope Poet Laureate (2011-2013) and is currently poetry editor for fungimag.com and sagegreenjournal.org

EGON GUNTHER lives as a poet and a painter in Upper Bavaria.

LAPO GUZZINI is a San Francisco-based translator, editor, and arts agitator. Until 2015 he ran The Emerald Tablet, an independent cultural venue. He has translated the poem of Sandro Sardella in this issue, and is completing a book of Sardella's poetry.

JACK HIRSCHMAN, who last year completed his life work defending the planet and building socialism, was both an emeritus Poet Laureate of San Francisco and co-founder of the Revolutionary Poets Brigade. A fourth volume of his classic *Arcanes* has been published this year.

EVERETT HOAGLAND lives in New Bedford, Massachusetts, has published five books, and his poetry has been published in The Progressive, Political Affairs, The Workers Weekly World, Spare Change, and in anthologies *Resisting Arrest, Stand Our Ground, What Saves Us, Ghost Fishing: An Eco-Justice Poetry Anthology, Liberation Poetry,* and *Afro Asia*.

ANTONELLA IASCHI was born in 1956 in Parma. She lives in Roccella Jonica on the coast of Calabria. She has written several books of poetry and many novels and plays. She started writing when she was 13, and she keeps on because she believes "narrating the street" is the only weapon to exist and to resist.

BRUCE ISAACSON is publisher of Zeitgeist Press. He is a Poet Laureate emeritus of Clark County, Nevada, a community of two million souls that encompasses Las Vegas and the Vegas Strip.

ZIBA KARBASSI was born in Tabriz, northwestern Iran and now lives in the UK. She has authored more than twelve books, both in her mother tongue and internationally. Her poetry has been translated into more than fifteen languages. In 2012, she was chosen by Contemporary Poetics Research Centre, Birkbeck, University of London, as one of the fifteen revolutionary poets in the world.

ELIOT KATZ is the author of seven books of poetry, including *Love, War, Fire, Wind and Unlocking the Exits*, as well as a prose book, *The Poetry and Politics of Allen Ginsberg*. Katz, whose late mother was a Holocaust survivor, has worked for many years as an activist for a wide range of peace and social-justice causes, including helping to create several housing and food programs for homeless families in New Jersey.

DANILO KOREN translated the poem by Antonella Iaschi.

D.L. LANG is an internationally published Jewish American poet who served as Poet Laureate of Vallejo, California from 2017-2019. Find her online at poetryebook.com

ANN LEONARD lives in Nashville, TN, where she has been an anti-death penalty activist and a paralegal on capital cases, as well as a writer on prison issues. While living in San Francisco, she won the city-wide Poets 11 contest in 2012 and 2014. She was a member of the Revolutionary Poets Brigade, published in their anthologies, read at their events, and was a featured poet at many Bay Area poetry readings.

GENNY LIM is the recipient of two Lifetime Achievement awards from PEN Oakland and Berkeley Poetry Festival. A San Francisco Jazz Poet Laureate emeritus, she is author of five poetry collections, *Winter Place, Child of War, Paper Gods and Rebels, KRA!, La Morte Del Tempo, and Island: Poetry and History of Chinese Immigrants on Angel Island,* winner of the American Book Award.

MARK LIPMAN, poet and multimedia artist, is the founder of Vagabond, the Culver City Small Press Book Festival and the Elba Poetry Festival; recipient of the 2015 Joe Hill Labor Poetry Award; winner of the 2016 International Latino Book Awards. He's been an outspoken critic of war and occupation and uses poetry to connect communities to the greater social issues, while building consciousness through the spoken word.

ANGELINA LLONGUERAS, born in Barcelona and a member of the Chicago and San Francisco Revolutionary Poets Brigades, recently published, *To My Friend Nathan Thornton: in Memoriam*, with a foreword by Jack Hirschman. Her poems have appeared in many anthologies. She translated Jack Hirschman's The Soviet Cenotaph Arcane into Catalan.

OSCAR LOCATELLI. In the '80s poet-editor of "abiti/lavoro" (clothes/work), a magazine of workers' writing; trade unionist, mayor for 10 years of Paladina, his hometown; currently president of Park of the Hills of Bergamo, Italy.

ANNA LOMBARDO lives in Venice. Poet, cultural activist, and freelance translator. Art director of the International Poetry festival "Palabra en el Mundo" in Venice. Bilingual poetic collections: *Even the fish are drunk* (2002); *No Alibi* (2004); *That Something Missing* (2009); *Con candide mani* (2020). Her poems are translated into multiple languages in national and

international journals and anthologies.
www.palabraenelmundo@wordpress.com

KIRK LUMPKIN is a poet, spoken word & performance artist, lyricist, and environmentalist. He's the author of two books of poetry, In *Deep* and *Co-Hearing* and two poetry/music CDs, The Word-Music Continuum and Sound Poems and has two CDs featuring his original rock songs, Positive Voodoo (with the Wild Buds) and Moondog Sessions.

JUAN ALCALA LUNA is the Filipino author of Washing Rice & Other Poems. These poems, written in English, are reflective of immediate exile, even as cultures are fused more than ever due to migrations and globalization. Some poems are symbolic of the Philippines, being on the crossroads of competing cultures from the East and the West.

BIPLAB MAJEE is a thinker, poet, prose writer, lit. critic, novelist and translator. So far he has more than 90 books in different subjects. He received 8 International, one Indian and 12 Local awards and honors. At present he is Chief-Advisor of ISISAR, Kolkata India.

devorah major is an art activist, poet, novelist, essayist, professor, mother, grandmother, friend, and lover of the earth and its peoples. Born and raised in California, she served as San Francisco's Third Poet Laureate (2002-2006).

AHCENE MARICHE was born in Tala Toulmouts in the commune of Tizi Rached, the region of the great poet Si Mohand U Mhand in the east of the city of Tizi Ouzou in greater Kabylia Algeria. He has published books of poetry in English, French, Berber, and Kybyle.

Chicago poet and educator **ELIZABETH MARINO** is with RPB/Chicago. Her chapbooks are *Debris* and *Ceremonies*. Her poem and memoir collection Asylum is forthcoming.

ÁNGEL L. MARTÍNEZ is a poet, musician, activist, and member of the New York Revolutionary Poets Brigade, and celebrating 27 years of The Bread is Rising Poetry Collective.

ALBERTO MASALA. Sardinian. Amoral. He thinks that poetry cannot speak about freedom. But be deeply ethical. That's why he thinks poetry must speak of liberation. He lives in Bologna.

TOMMI AVICOLLI MECCA is a queer, southern Italian poet, writer, and performer who was born and raised in a working-class home in South Philly, and now lives in San Francisco where he works fighting for tenants' rights and housing for all.

KAREN MELANDER-MAGOON is published in many anthologies, has sung major opera roles in Europe for two decades, and has five CDs online and video of her Lillie, A Musical. She is an interfaith minister and a co-editor of this anthology.

SARAH MENEFEE is a San Francisco poet and homeless movement activist. She is a founding member of the Revolutionary Poets Brigade, Revolutionaries for a New America and "First they came for the homeless." Her most recent books are *Human Star* and *CEMENT*, as well as various self-published volumes.

TUREEDA MIKELL is an activist for holism, and a storyteller weaving blood memory into medicine. She is the co-curator of *The Patrice Lumumba Anthology*, 2021, and author of *Synchronicity, The Oracle of Sun Medicine*, 2020, both released by Nomadic Press.

For **GAIL MITCHELL**, words are her foundation, and making a poem is part resistance, part fury. Emmett Till sits under her breastbone. History shatters her heart and poverty is a scathing rebuke, so she writes. It's the only way she can make sense of humanity's being inhumane.

ED MYCUE was born in an old Niagara Falls NY family, grew up in Texas, and worked as a gardener in France & in California. He is the author of *Mindwalking, selected poems* (Philos Press), *The Singing Man My Father Gave Me* (Menard Press), *Nightboats* (Minotur Press), and other chapbooks.

MAJID NAFICY, the Arthur Rimbaud of Persian poetry, fled Iran in 1983, a year and a half after the execution of his wife, Ezzat Tabaian in Tehran. He lives in Santa Monica.

BILL NEVINS lives in New Mexico. His books Heartbreak Ridge and Awe are in print from Swimming With Elephants Publications. He may be reached at bill_nevins@yahoo.com

BARBARA PASCHKE is a singer and a member of the Revolutionary Poets Brigade and the Roque Dalton Cultural Brigade. She translates from Spanish and French, and for this volume, she translated the poem of Francis Combes.

DOROTHY (DOTTIE) PAYNE is a poet, culture critic, painter, organizer, and international educator who has performed and exhibited throughout the world. She currently moves between her studios in St. Louis, Missouri and San Francisco's culturally vibrant Mission District where she ccontinures to perform, paint, and write.

POET E SPOKEN, AKA ELAINE BROWN, was born and raised in Brooklyn, New York. She's an activist, mother, history teacher, author of soon-to-be-released *Cried Out Laughing* "Never afraid to normalize conversations of trauma!"

GREGORY POND was born in Brooklyn to Panamanian parents, has written four books of poetry, is a member of the Revolutionary Poets Brigade, and facilitator of Poetically Speaking, a weekly conference-call program for seniors. He lives in San Francisco.

THORWALD PROLL, b. Kassel, Hesse, Germany 1941, became a member of the students' movement in 1966 in West Berlin. After two years in jail, he's published five books of poetry in German.

KATHY POWERS is a writer from Chicago who advocates for sustainability and expansion of accessible mental health services and public education about mental health.

JÖRG W. RADEMACHER, the translator of the poem of Egon Günther, is a biographer, editor, and translator, who composes occasional poems in three languages.

SANDRO SARDELLA is a poet and painter from Varese in northern Italy. Factory work and the political and avant-garde movements of the 1960/70s influence his work. He read his poems at the 2012 San Francisco International Poetry Festival.

LUIS FILIPE SARMENTO was born in Lisbon, 1956. Poet, journalist, translator, and film director, he has published over 30 books of poetry, fiction and essays. Some of his books and texts have been translated into 14 languages. He is the Coordinator for Portugal for the World Poetry Movement.

NINA SERRANO is a San Francisco Bay Area poet and producer of poetry radio programs on KPFA-fm and OZCAT radio FM. She also produces a multimedia series "Literary Dialogs with Nina Serrano."

KIM SHUCK is Poet Laureate Emerita of San Francisco, whose Laureate book, *Deer Trails,* was published by City Lights Books.

DINOS SIOTIS was born in Tinos, Greece, in 1944. He is editor of the literary magazines (de)kata and Poetix, runs the (de)kata publishing house, directs the Tinos International Literary Festival, and is currently president of the Greek Poets Circle.

DOREEN STOCK is a prodigious poet and activist, writer of *My Name is Y,* a memoir of an anti-nuclear demonstrator; she lives between Argentina and the SF Bay Area. Her other recent books are A Noise In The Garden (Kelsay Books, 2021), and *Your Excellency, Free Will* (translations of Amparo Casasbella Alconada, with Marcelo Holot), Prosa Amerian Editores, Argentina, 2021.

MATTHEW TALEBI is a poet who lives in the Los Angeles area.

SARAH THILYKOU is a Greek poet, translator, essayist, book reviewer, and editor. Her publications include *Duet of Islands, Kyoto 2018,* and *Angelic Flights,* New York 2021.

RAYMOND NAT TURNER, 'The Town Crier,' is a NYC poet privileged to have read at the Harriet Tubman Centennial Symposium; he is artistic director of JazzPoetry Ensemble, UpSurge!NYC, which has appeared at numerous festivals and venues including the Monterey Jazz Festival and Panafest in Ghana, West Africa.

OSCAR SAAVEDRA VILLAROEL, Chile, is a poet, professor, and video-poet, recipient of several international awards, member of World Poetry Movement, Director of Escuelas de Poesia and Festivale Internationale de Poesia.

DAVID VOLPENDESTA is a member of the Friends of Durruti, the Roque Dalton Cultural Brigade, and the San Francisco Revolutionary Poets Brigade. He is the author of *Forbidden Psalms* and is currently working on *Forbidden Psalms II*.

CATHLEEN WILLIAMS is a Sacramento poet and editor of the newspaper Homeward. She is also a member of the San Francisco RPB.

D. A. "ROARSHOCK" WILSON is a San Francisco poet, author of First Hours of a Rainy Day and Other Poems, and publisher of Roarshock Page, a literary street flier. He reads regularly, locally and internationally, in person and via the social web, and can be found online at his website. www.roarshock.net

XIAO XIAO 潇潇 is a Chinese poet and painter. She is the first Asian to receive the Tudor Arghezi International Poetry Prize of Romania, and Romania named her an honorary citizen.

JAMI PROCTOR XU is a bilingual poet and translator. She is the recipient of a Zhujiang Poetry Award and a First Readers Poetry Award. Her translations of Song Lin's collection, *Sunday Sparrows* (Zephyr, 2020), received the Northern California Book Award for Poetry in Translation.

ANDRENA ZAWINSKY is a Pittsburg born working-class poet who lives in Alameda, California; she is recipient of Oakland PEN and Josephine Miles Prize for her poetry.

REVOLUTIONARY POETS BRIGADE MISSION STATEMENT

NOW
As poets we are uniquely positioned to seize the possibilities of the time, bringing language to life and participating in the movement that is gathering as we speak...

IT'S TIME
Poetry has always been and continues to be not only the way the poet listens to his or her innermost being, but a way the spirit of the times, in its most forward-looking incarnation, is expressed and heard. And the times we're in, of crisis and the cry for transformation, particularly needs the news, as poet W.C. Williams said, "without which we die."

We say what we see: and that is the system that cannot rest until it extracts every drop from a desperate earth: capitalism. We say what we see: and that is the oppression of our class, driven to the streets and alleys of our cities, driven to the muddy fields, all because there is no profit in maintaining life and health. We are the harbingers of revolution and the awareness that underlies and drives it.

FOR THE REVOLUTIONARY POETS
In our common struggle toward freedom, each individual instinctively reaches for the best tool at hand. As artists, we have the most powerful tool of all, the ability to inspire, transform, and liberate, just in the nick of time as it happens, as the sick old ways rust, choke, sputter, and fade. Poets, those at the compressed razor-sharp edge of social thought, and all fellow artists of visionary courage, stay mindful of this historic opportunity, and lead with strong

revolutionary voice for all humankind to genuinely live and thrive in common spirit!

BRIGADE
Therefore, we want to create a Revolutionary Poets Brigade, to respond to the demands of the moment – provoking the future out of the confused minds of today, inspiring with the passion of the living word, in preparation for the development on a wider and larger scale of the uprising, the action that will overthrow this system of greed and exploitation.

As a network, we can be present and participate in the popular resistance that is going on around us by holding poetry events, by reading and speaking at demonstrations, and by publishing broadsides and pamphlets. Join us.

"Camerados . . . will you come travel with us? Shall we stick by each other as long as we live?"
–Walt Whitman

REVOLUTIONARY POETS BRIGADE
http://revolutionarypoetsbrigade.org

www.ingramcontent.com/pod-product-compliance
Lightning Source LLC
Chambersburg PA
CBHW032115090426
42743CB00007B/356